W9-AZF-460

Combining and Modifying SAS® Data Sets: Examples

Version 6
First Edition

SAS Institute Inc.
SAS Campus Drive
Cary, NC 27513

The correct bibliographic citation for this manual is as follows: SAS Institute Inc., *Combining and Modifying SAS® Data Sets: Examples, Version 6, First Edition*, Cary, NC: SAS Institute Inc., 1995. 197 pp.

Combining and Modifying SAS® Data Sets: Examples, Version 6, First Edition

Copyright © 1995 by SAS Institute Inc., Cary, NC, USA.

ISBN 1-55544-220-X

All rights reserved. Printed in the United States of America. No part of this publication may be reproduced, stored in a retrieval system, or transmitted, in any form or by any means, electronic, mechanical, photocopying, or otherwise, without the prior written permission of the publisher, SAS Institute Inc.

Restricted Rights Legend. Use, duplication, or disclosure by the U.S. Government is subject to restrictions as set forth in subparagraph (c)(1)(ii) of the Rights in Technical Data and Computer Software clause at DFARS 252.227-7013.

SAS Institute Inc., SAS Campus Drive, Cary, North Carolina 27513.

1st printing, August 1995

The SAS® System is an integrated system of software providing complete control over data access, management, analysis, and presentation. Base SAS software is the foundation of the SAS System. Products within the SAS System include SAS/ACCESS®, SAS/AF®, SAS/ASSIST®, SAS/CALC®, SAS/CONNECT®, SAS/CPE®, SAS/DMI®, SAS/EIS®, SAS/ENGLISH®, SAS/ETS®, SAS/FSP®, SAS/GRAPH®, SAS/IMAGE®, SAS/IML®, SAS/IMS-DL/I®, SAS/INSIGHT®, SAS/LAB®, SAS/NVISION®, SAS/OR®, SAS/PH-Clinical®, SAS/QC®, SAS/REPLAY-CICS®, SAS/SESSION®, SAS/SHARE®, SAS/SPECTRAVIEW®, SAS/STAT®, SAS/TOOLKIT®, SAS/TRADER®, SAS/TUTOR®, SAS/DB2™, SAS/GEO™, SAS/GIS™, SAS/PH-Kinetics™, SAS/SHARE*NET™, and SAS/SQL-DS™ software. Other SAS Institute products are SYSTEM 2000® Data Management Software, with basic SYSTEM 2000, CREATE™, Multi-User™, QueX™, Screen Writer™, and CICS interface software; InfoTap® software; NeoVisuals® software; JMP®, JMP IN®, JMP Serve®, and JMP *Design*® software; SAS/RTERM® software; and the SAS/C® Compiler and the SAS/CX® Compiler; VisualSpace™ software; and Emulus® software. MultiVendor Architecture™ and MVA™ are trademarks of SAS Institute Inc. SAS Institute also offers SAS Consulting®, SAS Video Productions®, Ambassador Select®, and On-Site Ambassador™ services. *Authorline*®, Books by Users™, The Encore Series™, *JMPer Cable*®, *Observations*®, *SAS Communications*®, *SAS Training*®, *SAS Views*®, the SASware Ballot®, and SelecText™ documentation are published by SAS Institute Inc. The SAS Video Productions logo and the Books by Users SAS Institute's Author Service logo are registered service marks and the Helplus logo and The Encore Series logo are trademarks of SAS Institute Inc. All trademarks above are registered trademarks or trademarks of SAS Institute Inc. in the USA and other countries. ® indicates USA registration.

The Institute is a private company devoted to the support and further development of its software and related services.

Other brand and product names are registered trademarks or trademarks of their respective companies.

Doc P4, 11JUL95

Contents

Your Turn

Credits

Documentation

Design and Production	Design, Production, and Printing Services
Style Programming	Publications Technology Development
Planning and Prototyping	Ginny Dunn, Amber Elam, Brenda C. Kalt, Carol Austin Linden, Rick Matthews, Denise J. Moorman, Lynn H. Patrick, and Helen Weeks
Programming	Ginny Dunn, Amber Elam, William F. Heffner, Charles A. Jacobs, Paul M. Kent, Susan Marshall, Rick Matthews, Denise J. Moorman, Lynn H. Patrick, Jon C. Schiltz, and Michael Williams
Writing and Editing	Deborah S. Blank, Carol Austin Linden, Patsy J. Poole, Philip R. Shelton, Helen Weeks, and John M. West
Technical Review	Ginny Dunn, Amber Elam, William F. Heffner, Kevin Hobbs, Charles A. Jacobs, Paul M. Kent, Susan Marshall, Rick Matthews, Denise J. Moorman, Lynn II. Patrick, Amy S. Peters, Jon C. Schiltz, Bruce Tindall, and Michael Williams

Recognition

This book was conceived and planned by members of the Technical Support and Publications Divisions. The SAS code was written by members of the Technical Support Division and of Research and Development. The book was reviewed by members of the Technical Support, Education, and Research and Development Divisions.

Without the advice, expertise, and skill in coding from members of other divisions within SAS Institute, this book would not have been possible. The Publications Division is grateful for the talent and expertise that helped create this book and would especially like to recognize the serious commitment of time and resources on the part of the Technical Support Division.

x

C H A P T E R   1

An Introduction to Data Relationships, Access Methods, and Techniques for Data Manipulation

Overview

Many applications, including Decision Support and Executive Information Systems, require input data to be in a specific format before it can be processed to produce meaningful results. Even if all of your data are already in SAS data sets, the data to support these systems typically come from multiple sources and may be in different formats. Therefore, you often, if not always, have to take intermediate steps to logically relate and process the data before you can analyze them or create reports from them.

Application requirements vary, but there are common denominators for all applications that access, combine, and process data. Once you have determined what you want the output to look like, you must

- □ discover how the input data are related
- □ select the appropriate access method to process the input data
- □ select the appropriate SAS tools to complete the task.

Data Relationships

Relationships among multiple sources of input data exist when the sources each contain common data, either at the physical or logical level. For example, employee data and department data could be related through an employee ID variable that shares common values. Another data set could contain numeric sequence numbers whose partial values logically relate it to a separate data set by observation number. Once data relationships exist, they fall into one of four categories:

- □ one-to-one
- □ one-to-many
- □ many-to-one
- □ many-to-many.

The categories are characterized by how observations relate among the data sets. All related data fall into one of these categories. You must be able to identify the existing relationships in your data since this knowledge is crucial to understanding how input data can be processed to produce desired results.

One-to-One

In a one-to-one relationship, typically a single observation in one data set is related to a single observation from another based on the values of one or more selected variables. A one-to-one relationship implies that each value of the selected variable occurs no more than once in each data set. When working with multiple selected variables, this relationship implies that each combination of values occurs no more than once in each data set.

***Figure 1.1* One-to-One**
Observations in SALARY and TAXES are related by common values for EMPNUM.

	SALARY		TAXES	
EMPNUM	SALARY		EMPNUM	TAXBRCKT
1234	55000		1111	0.18
3333	72000		1234	0.28
4876	32000		3333	0.32
5489	17000		4222	0.18
			4876	0.24

One-to-Many and Many-to-One

A one-to-many or many-to-one relationship between input data sets implies that one data set has at most one observation with a specific value of the selected variable but the other input data set may have more than one occurrence of each value. When working with multiple selected variables, this relationship implies that each combination of values occurs no more than once in one data set but may occur more than once in the other data set. The order in which the input data sets are processed determines whether the relationship is one-to-many or many-to-one.

***Figure 1.2* One-to-Many**
Observations in ONE and TWO are related by common values for variable A. Values of A are unique in data set ONE but not in TWO.

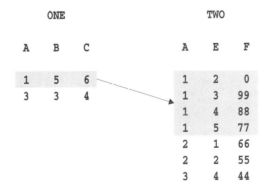

ONE				TWO		
A	B	C		A	E	F
1	5	6		1	2	0
3	3	4		1	3	99
				1	4	88
				1	5	77
				2	1	66
				2	2	55
				3	4	44

Figure 1.3 One-to-Many and
Many-to-One
Observations in data sets ONE, TWO, and
THREE are related by common values for
variable ID. Values of ID are unique in
ONE and THREE but not in TWO. For
values 2 and 3 of ID, a one-to-many
relationship exists between observations in
data sets ONE and TWO and a many-to-one
relationship exists between observations in
data sets TWO and THREE.

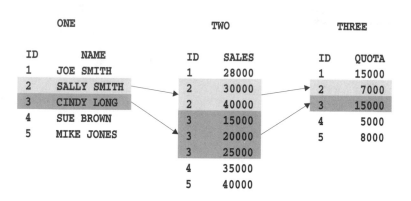

Many-to-Many

The many-to-many category implies that multiple observations from each
input data set may be related based on values of one or more common
variables.

Figure 1.4 Many-to-Many
Observations in data sets BREAKDWN and
MAINT are related by common values for
variable VEHICLE. Values of VEHICLE
are not unique in either data set. A
many-to-many relationship exists between
observations in these data sets for values
AAA and CCC of VEHICLE.

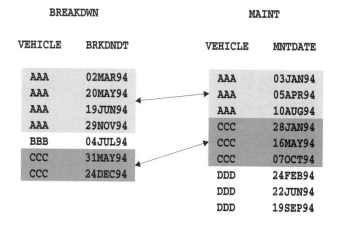

Access Methods: Sequential versus Direct

Once you have established data relationships, the next step is to determine the best mode of data access to *relate* the data. You can access observations sequentially in the order in which they appear in the physical file. Or you can access them directly, that is, you can go *straight to* an observation in a SAS data set without having to process each observation that precedes it.

Sequential Access

The simplest and perhaps most common way to process data with a DATA step is to read observations in a data set sequentially. You can read observations sequentially using the SET, MERGE, UPDATE, or MODIFY statements.

Direct Access

Direct access allows a program to access specific observations based on one of two methods:

□   by an observation number
□   by the value of one or more variables through a simple or composite index.

To access observations directly by their observation number, use the POINT= option with the SET or MODIFY statement. The POINT= option names a variable whose current value determines which observation a SET or MODIFY statement reads.

To access observations directly based on the values of one or more specified variables, you must first create an index for the variables and then read the data set using the KEY= option with the SET or MODIFY statement. An *index* is a separate structure that contains the data values of the key variable or variables paired with a location identifier for the observations containing the value.

An Overview of Methods for Combining SAS Data Sets

You can use these methods to combine SAS data sets:

□ concatenating

□ interleaving

□ one-to-one reading

□ one-to-one merging

□ match merging

□ updating.

Figures 1.5 through 1.9 show basic illustrations of all of these methods for combining SAS data sets.

Figure 1.5 Concatenating SAS Data Sets
Concatenating appends the observations from one data set to another data set.

DATA1 is read sequentially until all observations have been processed. Likewise, data sets in the SET statement are processed sequentially in the order in which they are listed.

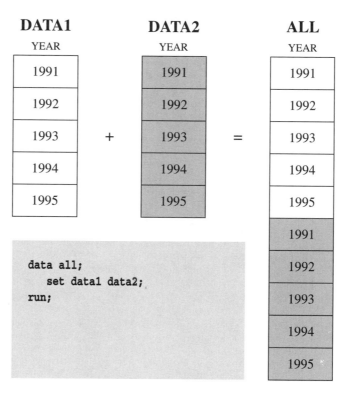

```
data all;
   set data1 data2;
run;
```

Figure 1.6   Interleaving
Interleaving intersperses observations from two or more data sets, based on one or more common variables.

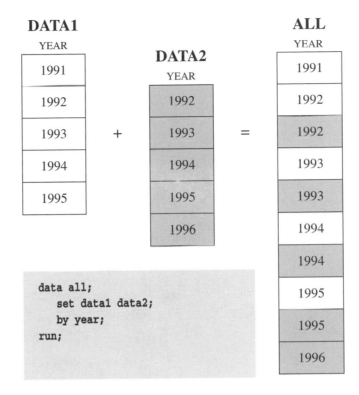

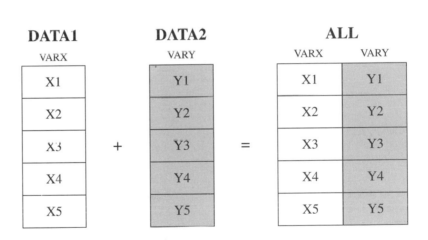

```
data all;
   set data1 data2;
   by year;
run;
```

Figure 1.7   One-to-One Reading or Merging
One-to-one reading combines observations from two or more data sets by creating observations that contain all of the variables from each contributing data set. Observations are combined based on their relative position in each data set, that is, the first observation in one data set with the first in the other, and so on.

The DATA step stops after it has read the last observation from the smallest data set.

One-to-one merging is the same as a one-to-one reading, with two exceptions: you use the MERGE statement instead of multiple SET statements, and the DATA step reads all observations from all data sets.

```
data all;
   set data1;
   set data2;
run;


data all;
   merge data1 data2;
run;
```

Figure 1.8 Match Merging
Match-merging combines observations from two or more data sets into a single observation in a new data set based on the values of one or more common variables.

DATA1	
YEAR	VARX
1991	X1
1992	X2
1993	X3
1994	X4
1995	X5

+

DATA2	
YEAR	VARY
1991	Y1
1991	Y2
1993	Y3
1994	Y4
1995	Y5

=

ALL		
YEAR	VARX	VARY
1991	X1	Y1
1991	X1	Y2
1992	X2	.
1993	X3	Y3
1994	X4	Y4
1995	X5	Y5

```
data all;
   merge data1 data2;
   by year;
run;
```

Figure 1.9 Updating

Updating uses information from observations in a transaction data set to delete, add, or alter information in observations in a master data set.

Note that MASTER and TRANS are both sorted by YEAR. Updating a data set requires that the data be sorted or indexed on the common variable. You can update a master data set by using the UPDATE statement or the MODIFY statement.

Note also that UPDATE and MODIFY do not replace nonmissing values in a master data set with missing values in a transaction data set.

MASTER

YEAR	VARX	VARY
1985	X1	Y1
1986	X1	Y1
1987	X1	Y1
1988	X1	Y1
1989	X1	Y1
1990	X1	Y1
1991	X1	Y1
1992	X1	Y1
1993	X1	Y1
1994	X1	Y1

TRANS

YEAR	VARX	VARY
1991	X2	•
1992	X2	Y2
1993	X2	•
1993	•	Y2
1995	X2	Y2

+ =

MASTER

YEAR	VARX	VARY
1985	X1	Y1
1986	X1	Y1
1987	X1	Y1
1988	X1	Y1
1989	X1	Y1
1990	X1	Y1
1991	X2	Y1
1992	X2	Y2
1993	X2	Y2
1994	X1	Y1
1995	X2	Y2

```
data master;
   update master trans;
   by year;
run;
```

An Overview of Tools for Combining SAS Data Sets

Once you understand the basics of establishing relationships among data, the ways to access data, and the ways you can combine SAS data sets, you can choose from a variety of SAS tools for accessing, combining, and processing your data. Table 1.1 lists and briefly describes the primary tools featured in this book.

Table 1.1 Tools for Combining SAS Data Sets

Statement or Proc	Action Performed	Access Method		Can Use with BY statement	Comments
		Sequential	Direct		
SET	reads an observation from one or more SAS data sets.	X	X	X	Use KEY= or POINT= for directly accessing data.
MERGE	reads observations from two or more SAS data sets and joins them into single observations.	X		X	When using MERGE with BY, the data must be sorted or indexed on the BY variable.
UPDATE	applies transactions to observations in a master SAS data set. UPDATE does not update observations in place; it produces an updated copy of the current data set.	X		X	Both the master and transaction data sets must be sorted by or indexed on the BY variable.
MODIFY	manipulates observations in a SAS data set in place. (Contrast with UPDATE.)	X	X	X	Sorted and indexed data are not required for direct access or use with BY, but are recommended for performance.
PROC SQL*	reads an observation from one or more SAS data sets; reads observations from up to 16 SAS data sets and joins them into single observations; manipulates observations in a SAS data set in place.	X	X	X	All three access methods are available in PROC SQL, but the access method is chosen by the internal optimizer.
BY	controls the operation of a SET, MERGE, UPDATE, or MODIFY statement in the DATA step and sets up special grouping variables.	NA	NA	NA	BY-group processing is a means of processing observations that have the same values of one or more variables.
IORC**	an automatic variable created when you use the MODIFY statement or when you use the SET statement with the KEY= option.	NA	NA	NA	The value of this variable is a numeric return code that indicates the status of the most recent I/O operation that used MODIFY or KEY=.
SYSRC**	an autocall macro that you use in conjunction with _IORC_ to test for specific I/O conditions.	NA	NA	NA	

* PROC SQL is the SAS System implementation of Structured Query Language. In addition to expected SQL capabilities, PROC SQL includes additional capabilities specific to SAS such as the use of formats and SAS macro language.

**_IORC_ and SYSRC are documented in detail in the Appendix.

Tools for Processing Information in Groups

BY-Group Processing

When combining SAS data sets, it is often convenient to process observations in BY-groups, that is, groups of observations that have the same value for one or more selected variables. Many examples in this book use BY-group processing with one or more SAS data sets to create a new data set.

The BY statement identifies one or more BY variables. When using the BY statement with the SET, MERGE, or UPDATE statement, your data must be sorted or indexed on the BY variable or variables.

In a DATA step, the SAS System identifies the beginning and end of each BY group by creating two temporary variables for each BY-variable: FIRST.*variable* and LAST.*variable*. These variables are set to 1 if true and 0 if false to indicate if that observation is the first or last in the current BY group. Using programming logic, you can test FIRST.*variable* and LAST.*variable* to determine if the current observation is the first, last, or both first and last in the current BY group. Testing the values of these variables in conditional processing lets you perform certain operations at the beginning or end of a BY group.

MODIFY and BY

Internally the MODIFY statement handles BY-group processing differently from the SET, MERGE, and UPDATE statements. MODIFY creates a dynamic WHERE clause, making it possible for you to use BY without either sorting or indexing your data first. However, processing based on FIRST.*variables* and LAST.*variables* can result in multiple BY groups for the same BY values if your data are not sorted. You may not, therefore, get the expected results unless you use sorted data. And even though sorting is not required, it is often useful for improved performance.

Array Processing

When you want to process several variables in the same way, use array processing. Processing variables in arrays can save you time and simplify your code. Use an ARRAY statement to define a temporary grouping of variables as an array. Then use a DO loop to perform a task repetitively on all or selected elements in the array.

Choosing between UPDATE and MODIFY

You can use either the UPDATE or MODIFY statement to update a master data set with information in a transaction data set. The UPDATE statement is a more familiar tool. Its only application is to update a master data set. MODIFY, a newer and more powerful tool, has many more applications. You can use the MODIFY statement to

□ process a file sequentially to apply updates in place (without a BY statement)

□ make changes to a master data set in place by applying transactions from a transaction data set

□ update the values of variables by directly accessing observations based on observation numbers

□ update the values of variables by directly accessing observations based on the values of one or more key variables.

Only one application of MODIFY is comparable to UPDATE: using MODIFY with the BY statement to apply transactions to a data set. While MODIFY is a more powerful tool than UPDATE, UPDATE is still the tool of choice in some cases. Table. 1.2 helps you choose whether to use UPDATE or MODIFY with BY.

Table 1.2   UPDATE versus MODIFY with BY

Issue	MODIFY with BY	UPDATE
Disk space	saves disk space because it updates data in place	requires more disk space because it produces an updated copy of the data set.
Sort and index	for good performance, it is strongly recommended that both data sets be sorted and that the master data set be indexed	requires only that both data sets be sorted
When to use	use only when you expect to process a SMALL portion of the data set	use if you expect to need to process most of data set
Duplicate BY-values	allows duplicate BY-values in both the master and transaction data sets	allows duplicate BY-values in only the transaction data set
Scope of changes	cannot change the data set descriptor information, so changes such as adding or deleting variables or variable labels, etc., are not valid	can make changes that require a change in the descriptor portion of a data set, such as adding new variables, etc.
Error-checking	has new error-checking capabilities using _IORC_ automatic variable and the SYSRC autocall macro	needs no error checking because transactions without a corresponding master record are not applied but are added to the data set
Data set integrity	data may only be partially updated due to an abnormal task termination	no data loss occurs because UPDATE works on a copy of the data

Where to Go from Here

The following sources contain more complete explanations of topics covered briefly in this chapter:

□ **Array processing and the ARRAY statement.** For a complete discussion, see pp. 160–171 in *SAS Language: Reference, Version 6, First Edition.* For a complete description of the ARRAY statement, see Chapter 9, "SAS Language Statements," in *SAS Language: Reference, Version 6, First Edition.* For a basic explanation and simple examples see Chapter 12, "Finding Shortcuts in Programming," in *SAS Language and Procedures: Usage, Version 6, First Edition.* For more extensive examples, see Chapters 7, 9, and 10 in *SAS Language and Procedures: Usage 2, Version 6, First Edition.*

□ **BY-group processing and the BY statement.** For a complete discussion, see pp. 131–136 in *SAS Language: Reference, Version 6, First Edition.* For a complete description of the BY statement, see Chapter 9, "SAS

Language Statements," in *SAS Language: Reference, Version 6, First Edition.*

☐ **Combining SAS Data Sets.** For a complete description and examples of concatenating, interleaving, one-to-one reading, one-to-one merging, match-merging, and updating, see pp. 137–160 in *SAS Language: Reference, Version 6, First Edition.* For more examples, see Part 4, "Combining SAS Data Sets," in *SAS Language and Procedures: Usage, Version 6, First Edition.*

☐ **Creating an index for a SAS data set.** For a discussion of indexes and how to create them, see pp. 217–225 in *SAS Language: Reference, Version 6, First Edition.* Also see the description of the INDEX= option in SAS Technical Report P-242, *SAS Software: Changes and Enhancements, Release 6.08*, pp. 31–32.

☐ **_IORC_ automatic variable and SYSRC autocall macro.** These error-checking tools were originally documented in SAS Technical Report P-222, *Changes and Enhancements to Base SAS Software, Release 6.07.* Both detailed descriptions and examples are in the appendix in this book. Also see Jacobs III, Charles A. (1992), "DATA Step Programming Using the MODIFY Statement," *Observations*, 2 (1), 4–11.

☐ **MERGE statement .** For complete reference documentation, see Chapter 9, "SAS Language Statements," in *SAS Language: Reference, Version 6, First Edition.*

☐ **MODIFY statement.** For complete reference documentation, see pages 1–10 in SAS Technical Report P-242, *SAS Software: Changes and Enhancements, Release 6.08.* Also see Jacobs III, Charles A. (1992), "DATA Step Programming Using the MODIFY Statement," *Observations*, 2 (1), 4–11.

☐ **PROC SQL procedure.** If you are unfamiliar with Structured Query Language, see *Getting Started with the SQL Procedure, Version 6, First Edition.* For complete documentation on PROC SQL, see *SAS Guide to the SQL Procedure: Usage and Reference, Version 6, First Edition.*

☐ **SET statement.** For complete reference documentation, see Chapter 9, "SAS Language Statements," in *SAS Language: Reference, Version 6, First Edition.* For information on the KEY= option, see p. 43 in SAS Technical Report P-222, *Changes and Enhancements to Base SAS Software, Release 6.07.* The UNIQUE option is described in SAS Technical Report P-242, *SAS Software: Changes and Enhancements, Release 6.08*, p. 14.

☐ **UPDATE statement.** For complete reference documentation, see Chapter 9, "SAS Language Statements," in *SAS Language: Reference, Version 6, First Edition.*

CHAPTER 2

Combining Single Observations with Single Observations

In a one-to-one relationship, typically a single observation in one data set is related to a single observation from another based on the value of a chosen variable. A one-to-one relationship implies that each value of this variable occurs only once in each data set.

Example 2.1

Merging Data Sets by a Common Variable, Specifying Their Origin, and Replacing Missing Values

Goal

Combine observations from two data sets based on a variable common to both. To make the new data set more informative, create a new variable whose values indicate the origin of each observation and replace the missing values that result from the merge operation with meaningful values.

Strategy

Use the MERGE and BY statements to *match-merge* the observations from two data sets. Use the IN= data set option to indicate which data sets contribute to an observation. Use IF-THEN/ELSE logic to specify the origin of the observation and to handle missing values that result from the merge operation. This task requires that each data set either have an index on the BY variable or be sorted by the values of the BY variable.

Input Data Sets

Both ONE and TWO are sorted by ID.

ONE

OBS	ID	NAME	DEPT	PROJECT
1	000	Miguel	A12	Document
2	111	Fred	B45	Survey
3	222	Diana	B45	Document
4	888	Monique	A12	Document
5	999	Vien	D03	Survey

TWO

OBS	ID	NAME	PROJHRS
1	111	Fred	35
2	222	Diana	40
3	777	Steve	0
4	888	Monique	37
5	999	Vien	42

Resulting Data Set

Output 2.1 COMBINE Data Set

COMBINE

OBS	ORIGIN	ID	NAME	DEPT	PROJECT	PROJHRS
1	one	000	Miguel	A12	Document	0
2	both	111	Fred	B45	Survey	35
3	both	222	Diana	B45	Document	40
4	two	777	Steve	NEW	NONE	0
5	both	888	Monique	A12	Document	37
6	both	999	Vien	D03	Survey	42

Program

The objective is to create a single data set that matches each individual with the correct departmental and project information based on corresponding ID values, to add a new variable indicating the origin of that information, and to add meaningful information where values are missing. This program match-merges the data sets ONE and TWO to create the data set COMBINE with the variables ID, NAME, DEPT, PROJECT, PROJHRS, and the new variable ORIGIN. Use the IN= data set option to determine which input data set contributes to the observation output to COMBINE. Use IF-THEN/ELSE logic to specify the values for ORIGIN. Use IF-THEN logic to supply meaningful values in the place of missing values that resulted from the merge.

Create COMBINE by merging observations from ONE and TWO based on the matching values for ID. IN= creates IN1, which is set to 1 when ONE contributes an observation, and IN2, which is set to 1 when TWO contributes an observation. ID is the BY variable.

```
data combine;
   length origin $ 4;
   merge one(in=in1) two(in=in2);
   by id;
```

Assign values to ORIGIN according to the specified conditions. Set the value of ORIGIN to indicate whether the current observation to be output to COMBINE received a contribution from data set ONE, data set TWO, or both data sets.

```
   if in1 and in2 then origin='both';
   else if in1 then origin='one';
   else origin='two';
```

Replace missing values with more meaningful values.

```
   if dept=' ' then dept='NEW';
   if project=' ' then project='NONE';
   if projhrs=. then projhrs=0;
run;
```

Example 2.2

Combining Observations When Variable Values Do Not Match Exactly

Goal

Perform a *fuzzy merge* by merging observations from two data sets based on data values that do not exactly match.

Strategy

Sort each data set by the variable you're comparing. Read an observation from each one, then compare the values of the appropriate variable. (Remember to rename variables common to both data sets so that values from one data set do not overwrite values from the other.) If the difference between the compared values is within an acceptable range, write an observation containing values from *both* data sets. If it isn't within an acceptable range, test to see which of the two observations should come first. Write to the data set an observation that contains those values, setting the values from the other input data set to missing to indicate that no appropriate match was found. Then read another observation from the data set that contributed the values you've just written to the output data set, and test again to see if you have a close match.

Because you need to read from one data set, from a second data set or from both based on the result of a comparison, there are three different points in the code from which you may need to execute a SET statement to read an observation. To simplify the code, put the SET statement in a group of statements following a label and use the LINK statement at each point in the program where a read should occur to branch execution to the appropriate SET statement. In each labeled group, precede the SET statement with an IF/THEN statement that prevents SET from attempting to read past the end of a data set. Otherwise, the DATA step might automatically end before all observations are processed from both data sets.

Use the END= variable to determine when you've read the last observation in a data set. Create another variable to indicate that an observation has been read *and* processed. Test the value of that variable for each data set so that you can end the DATA step only after the last observation has been read and processed from each input data set.

Using the SQL procedure, you can perform the same task with less code. See "Related Technique."

Note: Due to the variability of data and the number of conditions that determine the path chosen by the PROC SQL optimizer, it is not always possible to determine the most efficient method without first testing with your data.

Input Data Sets

Both ONE and TWO must be sorted by
TIME.

```
              ONE                               TWO

OBS         TIME        SAMPLE    OBS         TIME        SAMPLE

 1   23NOV94:09:01:00     100      1   23NOV94:09:00:00     200
 2   23NOV94:10:03:00     101      2   23NOV94:09:59:00     201
 3   23NOV94:10:58:00     102      3   23NOV94:11:04:00     202
 4   23NOV94:11:59:00     103      4   23NOV94:12:02:00     203
 5   23NOV94:13:00:00     104      5   23NOV94:14:01:00     204
 6   23NOV94:14:02:00     105      6   23NOV94:14:59:00     205
 7   23NOV94:16:00:00     106      7   23NOV94:15:59:00     206
                                   8   23NOV94:16:59:00     207
                                   9   23NOV94:18:00:00     208
```

Resulting Data Sets

Output 2.2a MATCH1 Data Set

MATCH1 was created with the DATA step.

```
                           MATCH1

OBS        TIME1            TIME2        SAMPLE1    SAMPLE2

 1    23NOV94:09:01    23NOV94:09:00       100       200
 2    23NOV94:10:03    23NOV94:09:59       101       201
 3    23NOV94:10:58          .             102        .
 4          .          23NOV94:11:04        .        202
 5    23NOV94:11:59    23NOV94:12:02       103       203
 6    23NOV94:13:00          .             104        .
 7    23NOV94:14:02    23NOV94:14:01       105       204
 8          .          23NOV94:14:59        .        205
 9    23NOV94:16:00    23NOV94:15:59       106       206
10          .          23NOV94:16:59        .        207
11          .          23NOV94:18:00        .        208
```

Output 2.2b MATCH2 Data Set

MATCH2 was created with PROC SQL.

```
                           MATCH2

OBS        TIME1        SAMPLE1        TIME2        SAMPLE2

 1    23NOV94:09:01       100     23NOV94:09:00       200
 2    23NOV94:10:03       101     23NOV94:09:59       201
 3    23NOV94:11:59       103     23NOV94:12:02       203
 4    23NOV94:14:02       105     23NOV94:14:01       204
 5    23NOV94:16:00       106     23NOV94:15:59       206
 6          .              .      23NOV94:11:04       202
 7          .              .      23NOV94:14:59       205
 8          .              .      23NOV94:16:59       207
 9          .              .      23NOV94:18:00       208
10    23NOV94:10:58       102           .              .
11    23NOV94:13:00       104           .              .
```

Program

The objective is to combine observations from data sets ONE and TWO when
the values of the variable TIME from both data sets are within five minutes of
each other. First, sort both data sets by TIME. Rename the variables TIME and
SAMPLE so that values do not overlay each other in the program data vector
when they are read from both data sets. Read an observation from each data
set, and write an observation to the MATCH data set if the values of TIME
meet the criteria. Then read again from each data set and continue comparing
values and writing observations when appropriate.

When the TIME values are not within five minutes of each other, test to determine which is earliest. Since the data are sorted by TIME, you know you won't find a closer match later in the other data set, so write an observation that contains the earliest TIME value and its associated SAMPLE value along with missing values to represent the other set of TIME and SAMPLE values. Then read again from the data set that contributed the earliest value, and again test to see if the match is close enough.

Prevent the DATA step from automatically ending when it reaches the end of the smallest data set by using an IF/THEN statement to test the value of a variable that indicates when the last observation is read. Because you have to prevent the SET statement from reading past the end of a data set *and* because you may need to read a new observation from data set ONE or TWO, or both data sets from multiple points in the program, you can place these statements in a labeled group and branch to it as appropriate:

Create MATCH1. Route execution to a group of statements that read an observation from ONE and then to another group that reads from TWO. Both groups prevent the DATA step from stopping before reaching the end of a data set.

```
data match1 (keep = time1 time2 sample1 sample2);
   link getone;
   link gettwo;
```

Format the datetime variables. Set to 0 the two variables that will be used to indicate that the last observation from data set ONE or TWO has been both read and processed. ONEDONE and TWODONE are not END= variables. The END= variables indicate only that the last observation has been *read*. These variables are set to 1 after the last observation has been *processed*.

```
   format time1 time2 datetime13.;
onedone=0;  twodone=0;
```

Check the value of TEMPT1 against TEMPT2. If there is less than a 5-minute (300-second) difference between them, assign the values of these "temp" variables to the variables that you want to write to the output data set, and then write an observation. Execute the LINK statements to read a new observation from ONE and from TWO. The ABS function returns the difference between TEMPT1 and TEMPT2 as a positive integer (regardless of which value is larger) so that you can compare them. Because this DO WHILE condition will always be true, this DATA step must be explicitly stopped later when processing is complete.

```
do while (1=1);
   if abs(tempt1-tempt2) < 300 then
      do;
         time1=tempt1;
         time2=tempt2;
         sample1=temps1;
         sample2=temps2;
         output;
         link getone;
         link gettwo;
      end;
```

If the difference between TEMPT1 and TEMPT2 is five minutes or more, test for further conditions. If the conditions are met, write an observation that contains the actual values from TWO but missing values from ONE. If the time value from ONE is greater than the time value from TWO *and* if the program has not already processed all observations from TWO, *or* if you have already reached the end of ONE, you know that you are not going to find a match for these values in data set ONE. So write an observation to MATCH that contains actual values from TWO and missing values from ONE. Then link to statements that read another observation from TWO so you can continue comparing.

```
else if (tempt1 > tempt2 and twodone=0) or onedone then
    do;
        time1=.;
        time2=tempt2;
        sample1=.;
        sample2=temps2;
        output;
        link gettwo;
    end;
```

If conditions have not been met in the previous IF-THEN or ELSE-IF/THEN statements, test for further conditions. If the conditions are met, write an observation that contains the actual values from ONE but missing values from TWO. This code segment uses the same logic as the previous one but writes values from ONE and links to statements that read another observation from ONE.

```
else if (tempt1 < tempt2 and onedone=0) or twodone then
    do;
        time1=tempt1;
        time2=.;
        sample1=temps1;
        sample2=.;
        output;
        link getone;
    end;
```

▨ *When you have processed all observations from both ONE and TWO, stop the DATA step.* Because the DO WHILE condition is always true, this DATA step must be explicitly stopped by this STOP statement.

```
    if onedone and twodone then stop;
    end;       /* ends the DO WHILE loop */
return;
```

If there are more observations in ONE, read another observation. If the last observation has already been read, set ONEDONE to 1 to indicate that the last observation was both read and processed and then prevent the SET statement from executing and attempting to read past the end of data set ONE. This strategy prevents the DATA step from ending automatically when there are no more observations to read. The RETURN statement causes execution to return to the LINK statement that branched execution to this label. Rename variables TIME and SAMPLE so that their values are not overwritten when variables of the same name are read from TWO. END= creates LAST1, a variable that is set to 1 when the last observation is read from ONE.

```
getone: if last1 then
            do;
                onedone=1;
                return;
            end;
        set one (rename=(time=tempt1 sample=temps1)) end=last1;
        return;
```

If there are more observations in TWO, read another observation. If the last observation has already been read, set TWODONE to 1 to indicate that the last observation was both read and processed, and then prevent the SET statement from executing and attempting to read past the end of data set TWO. This code segment uses the same logic as the previous one but applies to data set TWO.

```
gettwo: if last2 then
            do;
                twodone=1;
                return;
            end;
        set two (rename=(time=tempt2 sample=temps2)) end=last2;
        return;
run;
```

◪ A Closer Look

Stopping the DATA Step

You want to stop the DATA step after all observations have been *processed* from both data sets, *not* after all observations have been *read*. The END= variables, LAST1 and LAST2, are set to 1 after the last observation has been read. But the statements that *process* each observation are in a different location in the program from the SET statement and must operate conditionally based on whether the last observation has been *read and processed*, not just read. Otherwise, the last observation is read but never processed. To enable the last observation to be processed, the variables ONEDONE and TWODONE are created and are set to 1 only after the last observation in ONE and TWO, respectively, has been processed. The final IF-THEN statement in the program tests the variables ONEDONE and TWODONE and stops the DATA step when the values of both indicate that processing is complete.

Related Technique

The following PROC SQL step uses considerably less code to produce the same output as the DATA step, although the rows and columns are in a different order in the resulting data set.

PROC SQL joins the tables to produce a new table,[*] MATCH1. Conceptually, the join results in an internal table that matches every row in ONE with every row in TWO. The ON clause subsets that internal table by those rows where there is less than a five-minute time difference.

This join is a *full outer join*, which returns rows that satisfy the condition in the ON clause. In addition, a full outer join returns all of the rows from each table that do not match with a row from the other table, based on the condition in the ON clause. For example, for rows 202, 205, 207, and 208 in table TWO, there are no rows in table ONE that they can match with that results in a time differential of five minutes or less. Likewise, for rows 102 and 104 from table ONE, there are no rows in table TWO that they can match with that results in a time differential of five minutes or less.

---

[*]   A PROC SQL table is a SAS data set. In SQL terminology, columns are variables and rows are observations.

```
proc sql;
   create table match2 as
      select *
         from one(rename=(time=time1 sample=sample1)) full join
              two(rename=(time=time2 sample=sample2))
            on abs(time1-time2)<=5*60;
quit;
```

Note: In PROC SQL, SELECT *statements* automatically produce a report. SELECT *clauses*, which follow CREATE TABLE or CREATE VIEW statements, do not automatically produce a report.

Example 2.3

Combining Observations When There Is No Common Variable

Goal

Combine observations based on some criteria, even when there is no common variable in the two data sets.

Strategy

Use the looping action of the DATA step to access an observation from one data set on each iteration while reading all observations from a second data set to look for a match. To read the second data set, use the SET statement with the POINT= and NOBS= options in a DO loop to access all observations sequentially by observation number until a match is found. Then you can test a condition for each one to determine whether combining the information from the current observation of each data set is appropriate and write an observation to a new data set when the condition is met. Optionally, you can write a note to the SAS log when no match for a project is found.

You can perform the same task with PROC SQL, with the exception of writing a note to the log under a certain condition. See "Related Technique."

Note: Due to the variability of data and the number of conditions that determine the path chosen by the PROC SQL optimizer, it is not always possible to determine the most efficient method without first testing with the data.

Input Data Sets

The PROJECTS and BILLS data sets have no common variable. The dates associated with each project in PROJECTS do not overlap.

	PROJECTS				BILLS		
OBS	STDATE	ENDDATE	PROJECT	OBS	WORKID	COMPDATE	CHARGE
1	01/09/95	01/27/95	BASEMENT	1	1234	01/17/95	$944.80
2	02/01/95	02/12/95	FRAME	2	2225	02/18/95	$1,280.94
3	02/15/95	02/20/95	ROOFING	3	3879	03/04/95	$888.90
4	02/22/95	02/28/95	PLUMB	4	8888	03/21/95	$2,280.87
5	03/02/95	03/05/95	WIRE				
6	03/07/95	03/29/95	BRICK				

Resulting Data Sets

Output 2.3a COMBINE1 Data Set

COMBINE1 was created with the DATA step.

	COMBINE1					
OBS	PROJECT	STDATE	ENDDATE	WORKID	COMPDATE	CHARGE
1	BASEMENT	01/09/95	01/27/95	1234	01/17/95	$944.80
2	ROOFING	02/15/95	02/20/95	2225	02/18/95	$1,280.94
3	WIRE	03/02/95	03/05/95	3879	03/04/95	$888.90
4	BRICK	03/07/95	03/29/95	8888	03/21/95	$2,280.87

Output 2.3b COMBINE2 Data Set

COMBINE2 was created with PROC SQL.

```
                                  COMBINE2

  OBS    PROJECT     STDATE     ENDDATE    WORKID   COMPDATE     CHARGE

   1     BASEMENT    01/09/95   01/27/95    1234    01/17/95     $944.80
   2     ROOFING     02/15/95   02/20/95    2225    02/18/95   $1,280.94
   3     WIRE        03/02/95   03/05/95    3879    03/04/95     $888.90
   4     BRICK       03/07/95   03/29/95    8888    03/21/95   $2,280.87
```

Program

The objective is to bill charges to the correct phase of a construction project by creating a new data set that contains the appropriate information from PROJECTS and BILLS. Read each observation in PROJECTS and compare the values of the STDATE and ENDDATE variables to the value of COMPDATE in each observation in BILLS. If the completion date falls within the range of dates indicated by the project start and end date values, write an observation to COMBINE. Set FOUND to 1 and use that condition to stop the DO UNTIL loop so that no more observations are read from BILLS after a match is found.

Create COMBINE1. Read an observation from PROJECTS. Set FOUND back to 0. FOUND will be used to stop the DO UNTIL loop after a match has been found.

```
data combine1(drop=found);
   set projects;
   found=0;
```

Read observations from BILLS until a match is found or until all observations have been read. POINT= references a variable (I) whose value provides direct access to each observation in BILLS by observation number. NOBS= assigns the number of observations in BILLS to the variable N; the DO loop iterates once for each observation in BILLS until a match is found.

```
   do i=1 to n until (found);
      set bills point=i nobs=n;
```

When the condition is met, set FOUND to 1 and write an observation to COMBINE1. FOUND is set to 1 when a match is found. This condition stops the DO UNTIL loop so no more observations are read from BILLS on this iteration of the DATA step.

```
      if stdate <= compdate <= enddate then
         do;
            found=1;
            output;
         end;
   end;
```

If no observations match, write a note to the log.

```
   if not found then put 'No bills exist for: ' project
      'with start date ' stdate 'and enddate ' enddate +(-1) '.';
run;
```

Related Technique

If you are familiar with Structured Query Language (SQL), you may want to use PROC SQL instead of the DATA step. You cannot, however, write a note to the log under certain conditions as you can with the DATA step example.

PROC SQL joins the PROJECTS and BILLS tables to produce a new table,[*] COMBINE2. Conceptually, the join results in an internal table that matches every row in PROJECTS with every row in BILLS. Using that internal table, the WHERE clause determines that only the rows that have a value of COMPDATE that is between STDATE and ENDDATE will be in the resulting table.

```
proc sql;
   create table combine2 as
      select *
         from projects, bills
         where compdate between stdate and enddate;
quit;
```

Note: In PROC SQL, SELECT *statements* automatically produce a report. SELECT *clauses*, which follow CREATE TABLE or CREATE VIEW statements, do not automatically produce a report.

---

[*] A PROC SQL table is a SAS data set. In SQL terminology, columns are variables and rows are observations.

Example 2.4

Performing a Table Lookup When the Lookup Data Set is Indexed

Goal

Combine two data sets using a table lookup technique that directly accesses the lookup data set through an index on a *key* variable. This lookup technique is appropriate for a large lookup data set.

Strategy

Perform a table lookup using an index to locate observations that have key values equal to the current value of the key variable. Read from the primary file sequentially. To read the lookup data set, use the SET statement with the KEY= option to access the observations directly. Write all observations from the primary data set to the output data set even when no match is found and write a warning message to the SAS log. Before writing an observation, you can calculate a value for a new variable based on values from a variable in each data set. Use error-checking logic to direct execution to the appropriate code path.

You can perform the same task with PROC SQL, with the exception of writing a warning message to the SAS log when no match is found. See "Related Technique."

Note: Due to the variability of data and the number of conditions that determine the path chosen by the PROC SQL optimizer, it is not always possible to determine the most efficient method without first testing with the data.

Input Data Sets

EMPNUM is common to both the PRIMARY and LOOKUP data sets. PRIMARY contains no consecutive duplicate values for EMPNUM.* Because the program depends on directly accessing observations in LOOKUP by using KEY=EMPNUM, LOOKUP must be indexed on EMPNUM.

	PRIMARY			LOOKUP	
OBS	EMPNUM	SALARY	OBS	EMPNUM	TAXBRCKT
1	1234	$55,000	1	1111	0.18
2	3333	$72,000	2	1234	0.28
3	4876	$32,000	3	3333	0.32
4	5489	$17,000	4	4222	0.18
			5	4876	0.24

---

*   This program works as expected only if PRIMARY contains no consecutive observations with the same value for EMPNUM. For an explanation of the behavior of SET with KEY= when duplicates exist, see SAS Technical Report P-242, *SAS Software Changes and Enhancements, Release 6.08* page 14.

Resulting Data Sets

Output 2.4a FINAL1 Data Set

FINAL1 was created with the DATA step.

```
                              FINAL1

              OBS    EMPNUM    SALARY    TAXBRCKT      NET

               1      1234     $55,000     0.28      $39,600
               2      3333     $72,000     0.32      $48,960
               3      4876     $32,000     0.24      $24,320
               4      5489     $17,000       .           .
```

Output 2.4b FINAL2 Data Set

FINAL2 was created with PROC SQL.

```
                              FINAL2

              OBS    EMPNUM    SALARY    TAXBRCKT      NET

               1      1234     $55,000     0.28      $39,600
               2      3333     $72,000     0.32      $48,960
               3      4876     $32,000     0.24      $24,320
               4      5489     $17,000       .           .
```

Program

The objective is to create a new data set that includes all of the information from PRIMARY, only the corresponding descriptive information from LOOKUP, and the values of a new calculated variable. The resulting data set, FINAL1, contains the employee's number, salary, tax bracket, and net adjusted income.

First, read an observation from PRIMARY. Then use the SET statement with the KEY= option to read an observation from LOOKUP based on the current value of EMPNUM. To verify whether a matching value in LOOKUP has been located for the current value of EMPNUM in PRIMARY, use the %SYSRC autocall macro and the _IORC_ automatic variable.[*] When a match is found, calculate a value for NET based on the current values of SALARY from PRIMARY and TAXBRCKT from LOOKUP. When no match is found, set TAXBRCKT to missing and write a message to the SAS log.

Create FINAL1. Read an observation from PRIMARY.

```
data final1;
   set primary;
```

Read an observation from LOOKUP based on the value of the key variable, EMPNUM. The SET statement with KEY= accesses an observation directly through the index, using the current value of EMPNUM.

```
   set lookup key=empnum;
```

---

[*]   _IORC and SYSRC are documented in detail in the Appendix.

When an observation from LOOKUP has been successfully located and retrieved, calculate a value for NET. When the value of _IORC_ corresponds to _SOK, the value of EMPNUM in the observation retrieved from LOOKUP matches the current EMPNUM value from PRIMARY.*

When no match is found, set TAXBRCKT to missing and write a warning message to the SAS log. When the value of _IORC_ corresponds to _DSENOM, no observations in LOOKUP contain the current value of EMPNUM. If you do not set TAXBRCKT to missing when no match is found, the value from the observation most recently retrieved from LOOKUP is written as part of the current observation. _ERROR_ is reset to 0 to prevent an error condition that would write the contents of the program data vector to the SAS log.

In case of an unexpected _IORC_ condition, write an error message and stop execution. When _IORC_ corresponds to anything other than _DSENOM or _SOK, an unexpected condition has been met, so an error message is written to the SAS log and the STOP statement executes to terminate the DATA step.

```
select(_iorc_);
   when (%sysrc(_sok))
      do;
         net=salary*(1-taxbrckt);
      end;


   when (%sysrc(_dsenom))
      do;
         taxbrckt=.;
         put 'WARNING: No tax information for empnum ' empnum;
         _error_=0;
      end;







   otherwise
      do;
         put 'Unexpected ERROR:  _IORC_ =  ' _iorc_;
         stop;
      end;
   end;      /* ends the SELECT group */
run;
```

---

* _IORC and SYSRC are documented in detail in the Appendix.

Related Technique

If you are familiar with Structured Query Language (SQL), you may want to use PROC SQL instead of the DATA step. PROC SQL joins the tables to produce a new table,* FINAL2. Conceptually, the join results in an internal table that matches every row in PRIMARY with every row in LOOKUP. The ON clause subsets that internal table to include only these rows for employees who are in both tables.

This join is a *left outer join*, which returns rows that satisfy the condition in the ON clause. In addition, a left outer join returns all of the rows from the left table (first table listed in the FROM clause) that do not match with a row from the right table (second table listed in the FROM clause). Thus, the resulting table has a row for employee 5489, even though there is no row for 5489 in the LOOKUP table.

```
proc sql;
   create table final2 as
      select primary.empnum,primary.salary,taxbrckt,
             salary*(1-taxbrckt) as net format=dollar7.
         from primary left join lookup
            on primary.empnum=lookup.empnum;
quit;
```

Note: In PROC SQL, SELECT *statements* automatically produce a report. SELECT *clauses*, which follow CREATE TABLE or CREATE VIEW statements, do not automatically produce a report.

---

* A PROC SQL table is a SAS data set. In SQL terminology, columns are variables and rows are observations.

Example 2.5

Performing a Table Lookup When the Lookup Data Set is Not Indexed

Goal

Subset the observations from one data set into one of two output data sets, based on specified criteria.

Strategy

Load into an array the data that will be used to determine in which subset an observation belongs. Read the input data set sequentially, performing a lookup into the array structure. Compare values in the current observation to the appropriate values from the array to determine whether they fall within a specified range. Then write the current observation to the appropriate output data set.

Input Data Sets

BTEAM contains data on team members' height, weight, and body type. IDEAL shows the ideal male weight for each height, based on one of three body types. IDEAL is loaded into an array.

BTEAM

OBS	LNAME	SEX	HEIGHT	WEIGHT	TYPE
1	Adams	M	67	160	2
2	Alexander	M	69	115	1
3	Apple	M	69	139	1
4	Arthur	F	66	125	2
5	Avery	M	66	152	2
6	Barcfoot	M	68	158	2
7	Baucom	M	70	170	3
8	Blair	M	69	133	1
9	Blalock	M	68	148	2
10	Bostic	F	74	170	3

IDEAL

OBS	HEIGHT	SMALL	MEDIUM	LARGE
1	66	126	138	149
2	67	130	141	154
3	68	134	145	158
4	69	138	149	162
5	70	142	153	167
6	71	146	157	172
7	72	150	161	177
8	73	154	165	181
9	74	158	169	185
10	75	162	173	189

Resulting Data Sets

Output 2.5a INSHAPE Data Set

```
                              INSHAPE

              OBS    HEIGHT    LNAME     WEIGHT   TYPE

               1       69      Apple      139       1
               2       70      Baucom     170       3
               3       69      Blair      133       1
               4       68      Blalock    148       2
```

Output 2.5b OUTSHAPE Data Set

```
                              OUTSHAPE

              OBS    HEIGHT    LNAME       WEIGHT   TYPE

               1       67      Adams        160      2
               2       69      Alexander    115      1
               3       66      Avery        152      2
               4       68      Barefoot     158      2
```

Program

The objective is to create subsets from the BTEAM data set, based on whether a male team member is considered to be in shape or out of shape. The IDEAL data set contains three WEIGHT values for each HEIGHT, based on an ideal male weight for each body TYPE. These values are used to determine whether an observation from the BTEAM data set should be written to the INSHAPE or OUTSHAPE data set.

So that all of the values from IDEAL are available for comparing to the WEIGHT value in each observation in BTEAM, load values from IDEAL into a temporary array. A subsetting IF statement ensures that the only observations processed are those for males with values for HEIGHT and WEIGHT that are within a specified range. Use expressions to determine if a WEIGHT value is within a range of five pounds above or below the ideal weight for that body type. IF-THEN, ELSE, and OUTPUT statements write each observation to the appropriate data set.

Create INSHAPE and OUTSHAPE.

```
data inshape outshape;
   keep lname height weight type;

   array wt(66:75,3) _temporary_;
   if _n_=1 then
      do i=1 to all;
         set ideal nobs=all;
         wt(height,1)=small;
         wt(height,2)=medium;
         wt(height,3)=large;
      end;
```

■ *On the first DATA step iteration, load a two-dimensional temporary array from the information in IDEAL.* The DO loop reads each observation from IDEAL and loads the WT array. The assignment statements assign weight values from IDEAL to the correct array cells. There are three weight values for each height, one for each of three frame sizes. Note that the bounds of the first dimension of WT are 66 and 75, the smallest and largest HEIGHT values in inches.

Read an observation from BTEAM.

```
set bteam;
```

Determine whether a male qualifies as in shape or out of shape and write the observation to INSHAPE or OUTSHAPE.
The subsetting IF statement allows only observations for males to be processed. The other conditions ensure that TYPE and HEIGHT are valid values for this application. Otherwise, invalid values might be used to locate values in the array, causing an error that would terminate the DATA step. The IF-THEN statement writes to INSHAPE each observation that meets the criteria. The ELSE statement writes all other observations to OUTSHAPE.

```
if sex='M'and 3 ge type ge 1 and 75 ge height ge 66;
if wt(height,type)-5 le weight le wt(height,type)+5
   then output inshape;
else output outshape;
run;
```

⬛ A Closer Look

Processing the Two-Dimensional Array WT

To help you visualize processing in this example, Figure 2.1 represents the two-dimensional array WT, beginning with the lower bound of 66. If you compare it to the IDEAL data set, you can see how it was constructed.

Figure 2.5 Representation of Two-Dimensional Array WT

		HEIGHT									
		66	67	68	69	70	71	72	73	74	75
T											
Y	1	126	130	134	138	142	146	150	154	158	162
P	2	138	141	145	149	153	157	161	165	169	173
E	3	149	154	158	162	167	172	177	181	185	189

This statement processes the array:

```
if wt(height,type)-5 le weight le wt(height,type)+5
   then output inshape;
else output outshape;
```

On the first iteration of the DATA step, the first observation from BTEAM is processed:

```
Adams M 67 160 2
```

The cell in the array that is the intersection of column 67 (HEIGHT) and row 2 (TYPE) contains the weight value 141. The IF-THEN statement processes these values:

```
if (141-5) le 160 le (141+5)
   then output inshape;
else output outshape;
```

Temporary Arrays

When elements in an array are constants that are only needed during the duration of the DATA step, you can save execution time by using temporary arrays instead of creating variables, as shown in this ARRAY statement:

```
array wt(66:75,3) _temporary_;
```

In addition to saving execution time, temporary array elements differ from variables in the following ways:

□   They are not written to the output data set.

□   They do not have names and can be referenced only by their array names and dimensions.

□   They are automatically retained, instead of reset to missing, at the beginning of the DATA step.

Where to Go from Here

□   **Two-Dimensional Arrays.** For a discussion, see pp. 165–169 in *SAS Language: Reference, Version 6, First Edition.* For examples, see Chapter 7, "Grouping Variables to Perform Repetitive Tasks Easily," in *SAS Language and Procedures: Usage 2, Version 6, First Edition* and Example 14, "Expense Report," in *SAS Guide to Report Writing: Examples, Version 6, First Edition.*

□   **Temporary Array Elements.** For an explanation and an example, see pp. 129–131 in *SAS Language and Procedures: Usage 2, Version 6, First Edition.* For a short example, see pp. 170–171 in *SAS Language: Reference, Version 6, First Edition.*

Example 2.6

Matching Observations Randomly

Goal

Randomly pair observations from transaction and master data sets until a good match is found. Create a new data set containing the results of the match. Update the value of a variable in the master data set appropriately.

Strategy

Sequentially process observations from the transaction data set. Access the master data set directly by observation number, using the MODIFY statement with the POINT= and NOBS= options; MODIFY allows the data set to be updated in place. Use the RANUNI function to randomly generate a number, and use the CEIL function to return it as an integer; assign the resulting integer to the POINT= variable. Use IF-THEN logic to test a variable for a condition. Continue reading observations until one meets the condition, write an observation to a new data set, assign a value to a new variable, and update a value in the master data set.

Input Data Sets

```
        ENGINEER                      PROJECTS

OBS   ENGINEER   AVAILHRS       OBS   PROJID   HOURS
 1      Inge        33           1    AERO       31
 2      Jane       100           2    BRANDX    150
 3     Eduardo      12           3    CHEM       18
 4      Fred        16           4    CONTRA     41
 5      Kia        130           5    ENG2        6
 6     Monique      44           6    ENG3       29
 7      Sofus       23
```

Resulting Data Sets

Output 2.6a Updated Version of ENGINEER Data Set

```
              ENGINEER

OBS    ENGINEER    AVAILHRS
 1      Inge          33
 2      Jane          82
 3     Eduardo         6
 4      Fred          16
 5      Kia           60
 6     Monique        13
 7      Sofus         23
```

Output 2.6b ASSIGN Data Set

```
              ASSIGN

OBS    PROJID    ENGINEER
 1      Aero      Monique
 2      Brandx    NONE
 3      Chem      Jane
 4      Contra    Kia
 5      Eng2      Eduardo
 6      Eng3      Kia
```

Program

The data set ENGINEER lists engineers and their available hours. The data set PROJECT lists each project by ID and the hours needed to complete that project. The objective is to use a random direct access technique to match a project with an engineer who has sufficient hours to complete that project, output the results to the new data set ASSIGN, and update ENGINEER to reflect the hours remaining for each engineer after assignment. The random direct access technique causes the program to produce different output each time it is executed.

Read an observation from PROJECTS sequentially. Use the RANUNI and CEIL functions to generate a random integer and assign its value to X, the POINT= variable. This value is the observation number. Use IF-THEN logic to write an observation to ASSIGN when the engineer hours equal or exceed the hours needed to complete the task. The DO loop continues iterating until one engineer is selected for a project. Decrease the engineer's available hours by the value of HOURS, and use the REPLACE statement to update ENGINEER accordingly.

FOUND is then set to 1 and the next project is accessed. Exiting the loop when FOUND=0 means that no engineer with sufficient hours was found and, therefore, assigns the value 'NONE' to ENGINEER and writes an observation to ASSIGN.

Open ENGINEER for update and create ASSIGN. Read an observation from PROJECTS.

```
data engineer assign(keep=engineer projid);
   set projects;
   found=0;
```

Process observations from ENGINEER until an engineer is selected for the current project or until it iterates 1,000 times.

```
   do i=1 to 1000 while (not found);
```

Generate random values that will be used to access ENGINEER by observation number and assign the results to the variable X. The RANUNI function randomly generates numbers and returns a value based on a seed. Multiplying that value by the number of engineers (N) and then using the CEIL function returns an integer between 1 and N.

```
      x=ceil(ranuni(12345)*n);
```

Use the value of X to access observations in ENGINEER by observation number. POINT= uses the variable X, whose value provides direct access to observations in ENGINEER by observation number. NOBS= assigns the number of observations in ENGINEER to N.

```
      modify engineer point=x nobs=n;
```

When the available engineering hours exceed or equal the hours needed to complete the project, write the observation to ASSIGN, calculate a new value for AVAILHRS, and update ENGINEER. The assignment statement assigns a new value to AVAILHRS, and the REPLACE statement updates the current observation read from ENGINEER with the new value for AVAILHRS. FOUND is set to 1, so the DO loop will stop because an engineer has been selected.

```
    if availhrs>=hours then
        do;
            output assign;
            availhrs=availhrs-hours;
            replace engineer;
            found=1;
        end;
end;      /* ends the iterative DO loop */
```

When no engineer's available hours equal or exceed the hours needed for the current project, write an observation to ASSIGN indicating that no engineer was assigned.

```
    if found=0 then do;
        engineer="NONE";
        output assign;
    end;
run;
```

Example 2.7

Combining Observations Based on a Calculation on Variables Contributed by Two Data Sets

Goal

Use one-to-many matching on columns* in two tables and perform a calculation that shows the relationship between values in columns that are unique to each table. Produce a table that includes only those rows that meet a specified condition.

Strategy

Use the SQL procedure to join two tables. The join produces a *Cartesian product*, which is a combination of each row from the first table with every row from the second table. During the join, you can perform mathematical computations to create a new column using values from columns that are common to both tables. Subset the join to get only those rows that have a specified value of the new column.

Input Data Sets

ONE

OBS	HOUSE	X	Y
1	house1	1	1
2	house2	3	3
3	house3	2	3
4	house4	7	7

TWO

OBS	STORE	X	Y
1	store1	6	1
2	store2	5	2
3	store3	3	5
4	store4	7	5

Resulting Data Set

Output 2.7 FINAL Table

FINAL

OBS	HOUSE	Closest Store	Distance
1	house1	store2	4.12
2	house2	store3	2.00
3	house3	store3	2.24
4	house4	store4	2.00

---

* A PROC SQL table is a SAS data set. In SQL terminology, columns are variables and rows are observations.

Program

The objective is to join ONE and TWO to get a row for every combination of house and store. In this example, the join results in an internal table of 16 rows, four for each house.

For each row, calculate the distance between each house and each store by performing mathematical calculations on the X and Y coordinates. Lastly, determine which store is closest to each house. Select only those rows whose values for DIST represent the minimum distance from a specific house to the closest store.

Invoke PROC SQL and create a table. The CREATE TABLE statement creates the table FINAL to store the results of the subsequent query.

```
proc sql;
   create table final as
```

Select the columns. The SELECT clause selects the HOUSE and STORE columns from tables ONE and TWO, respectively.

```
      select one.house, two.store label='Closest Store',
```

■ *Calculate a new column.* The arithmetic expression uses the square root function (SQRT) to create an additional column, DIST, that contains the distance from HOUSE to STORE for each row.

```
         sqrt((abs(two.x-one.x)**2)+(abs(two.y-one.y)**2)) as dist
            label='Distance' format=4.2
```

Name the tables to join and query.

```
      from one,two
```

Group the data by values of HOUSE and subset the grouped data. The HAVING clause subsets the grouped data by selecting the row with the lowest value for DIST from each group. CALCULATED takes the place of the mathematical expression that calculates the values of DIST.

```
      group by house
      having calculated dist= min(dist.);
quit;
```

Note: In PROC SQL, SELECT *statements* automatically print output. SELECT *clauses*, which follow CREATE TABLE or CREATE VIEW statements, do not automatically print output.

◪ A Closer Look

Calculate a New Column

It may help you to visualize the plot of the location of the houses and stores and to actually see how the distance between a specific house and store is calculated. The following plot shows the position of each house and store:

Figure 2.7 Plot Showing Position of Houses and Stores

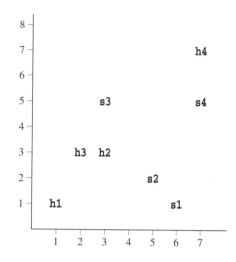

As an example, this is the calculation for the distance between `house1` and `store1`:

```
sqrt((abs(two.x-one.x)**2)+(abs(two.y-one.y)**2))
   sqrt((abs(6   -  1)**2)+(abs(  1  -   1)**2))
        sqrt((5**2)        +        (0**2))
            sqrt(25        +          0)
                 sqrt(25)
                         =5
```

Note: A double asterisk (**) represents exponentiation.

C H A P T E R 3

Combining a Single Observation with Multiple Observations

A one-to-many or many-to-one relationship between input data sets implies that specific values of one or more chosen variables are unique in one data set but may occur in multiple observations in the other data set. The order in which the input data sets are processed determines whether the relationship is one-to-many or many-to-one.

Example 3.1

Adding Values to All Observations in a Data Set

Goal

Efficiently combine values from a single observation in one data set with all observations in another data set.

Strategy

On the first iteration of the DATA step, read the values of all variables from a single observation in one data set once to place those values into the program data vector. Then read each observation in the second data set, outputting a new observation that contains the combined values.

Input Data Sets

Each salesperson in SALESREP works in the store and department identified in DEPT_ID.

	DEPT_ID			SALESREP		
OBS	STORE	DEPT	OBS	NAME	MONTH	TOTSALES
1	13	VIDEO	1	Harvey	Jan	$25,375
			2	Lou	Jan	$9,950
			3	Mary	Jan	$27,985
			4	Sam	Jan	$8,795

Resulting Data Set

Output 3.1 SALES_ID Data Set

	SALES_ID					
OBS	STORE	DEPT	NAME	MONTH	TOTSALES	
1	13	VIDEO	Harvey	Jan	$25,375	
2	13	VIDEO	Lou	Jan	$9,950	
3	13	VIDEO	Mary	Jan	$27,985	
4	13	VIDEO	Sam	Jan	$8,795	

Program

The objective is to take the data set that contains information about sales representatives and add to each observation the same values for two new variables, STORE and DEPT. The only observation in DEPT_ID contains values for STORE and DEPT. The IF-THEN statement with the _N_ option executes the SET statement to read from DEPT_ID only once, on the first iteration of the DATA step. The values for STORE and DEPT remain in the program data vector for the duration of the DATA step execution because values read with the SET statement are automatically retained until another observation is read from that data set. Each iteration reads an observation from SALESREP and writes an observation that contains the same value for STORE and DEPT and all the data for a single sales representative:

Create SALES_ID. Read an observation from DEPT_ID only on the first iteration. Since DEPT_ID contains only one observation, using IF-THEN and _N_ to read from it only once avoids prematurely ending the DATA step when end-of-file is reached. The variable values from DEPT_ID are retained throughout the DATA step.

```
data sales_id;
   if _n_=1 then set dept_id;
```

Read an observation from SALESREP and automatically write an observation to SALES_ID.

```
   set salesrep;
run;
```

Example 3.2

Adding Values from the Last Observation in a Data Set to All Observations in Another Data Set

Goal

Efficiently combine values from the last observation in one data set to all observations in another data set.

Strategy

Read the values of all variables from the last observation in one data set once to place those values into the program data vector. You can use the POINT= and NOBS= options with the SET statement to go directly to the last observation in the data set. Then read each observation in the second data set, writing a new observation that contains the combined values.

Input Data Sets

Each salesperson in SALESREP works in the store and department shown in the last observation in DEPT_ID.

	DEPT_ID			SALESREP		
OBS	STORE	DEPT	OBS	NAME	MONTH	TOTSALES
1	02	AUTO	1	Harvey	Jan	$25,375
2	07	HSEWARES	2	Lou	Jan	$9,950
3	10	AUDIO	3	Mary	Jan	$27,985
4	13	VIDEO	4	Sam	Jan	$8,795

Resulting Data Set

Output 3.2   SALES_ID Data Set

			SALES_ID		
OBS	STORE	DEPT	NAME	MONTH	TOTSALES
1	13	VIDEO	Harvey	Jan	$25,375
2	13	VIDEO	Lou	Jan	$9,950
3	13	VIDEO	Mary	Jan	$27,985
4	13	VIDEO	Sam	Jan	$8,795

Program

The objective is to take the data set that contains information about sales representatives and add to each observation the same value for store and department, which are read from another data set. The last observation in DEPT_ID contains the correct store and department values, so that observation is read on the first iteration of the DATA step. The values for STORE and DEPT remain in the program data vector for the duration of the DATA step execution because values read with the SET statement are automatically retained until other values for those same variables are read to replace them. Each DATA step iteration reads an observation from SALESREP and writes an observation that contains the same value for STORE and DEPT and all of the data for a single sales representative:

Create SALES_ID. Read the last observation from DEPT_ID on the first iteration. NOBS= sets the value of LAST to 4, the last observation in the data set. POINT= allows you direct access to observation 4.

```
data sales_id;
   if _n_=1 then set dept_id point=last nobs=last;
```

Read an observation from SALESREP and automatically write an observation to SALES_ID.

```
   set salesrep;
run;
```

Example 3.3

Merging Observations from Multiple Data Sets Based on a Common Variable

Goal

Combine observations from multiple data sets based on a variable common to each contributing data set. This task requires that each data set either have an index on the BY variable or be sorted by the values of the BY variable.

Strategy

Use the BY statement and the MERGE statement to *match-merge* the observations whose data sets are specified in the MERGE statement by the values of the BY variable.

Input Data Sets

The data sets must be sorted by the values of ID. Each value of ID occurs only once in data sets ONE and THREE but may occur multiple times in TWO.

ONE

OBS	ID	NAME
1	1	Nay Rong
2	2	Kelly Windsor
3	3	Julio Meraz
4	4	Richard Krabill
5	5	Rita Giuliano

TWO

OBS	ID	SALE
1	1	$28,000
2	2	$30,000
3	2	$40,000
4	3	$15,000
5	3	$20,000
6	3	$25,000
7	4	$35,000
8	5	$40,000

THREE

OBS	ID	BONUS
1	1	$2,000
2	2	$4,000
3	3	$3,000
4	4	$2,500
5	5	$2,800

Resulting Data Set

Output 3.3 FINAL Data Set

FINAL

OBS	ID	NAME	SALE	BONUS
1	1	Nay Rong	$28,000	$2,000
2	2	Kelly Windsor	$30,000	$4,000
3	2	Kelly Windsor	$40,000	$4,000
4	3	Julio Meraz	$15,000	$3,000
5	3	Julio Meraz	$20,000	$3,000
6	3	Julio Meraz	$25,000	$3,000
7	4	Richard Krabill	$35,000	$2,500
8	5	Rita Giuliano	$40,000	$2,800

Program

Create FINAL. Combine observations from the three data sets based on the matching values for ID to create the FINAL data set.

The objective is to create a new data set that matches each individual with the correct sale and bonus based on corresponding ID values. This program match-merges the data sets ONE, TWO, and THREE to create a single data set that contains variables ID, NAME, SALE, and BONUS:

Data set TWO contains multiple occurrences of some values of ID, while ONE and THREE contain only one occurrence. Because values of NAME and BONUS (which are read from ONE and THREE) are automatically retained across the BY group, multiple observations with the same value for ID contain the correct NAME and BONUS values:

```
data final;
   merge one two three;
   by id;
run;
```

Example 3.4

Applying Transactions to a Master Data Set Based on a Common Variable

Goal

Use a common variable to update the values of variables in a master data set with the values of variables in a transaction data set without writing missing values to the revised master data set and without overlaying variable values in the program data vector.

Strategy

Use the MERGE and BY statements to update the values of a master data set with the values of a transaction data set. Use the IN= data set option to indicate whether the transaction data set contributed to this observation. If it did not contribute, use IF-THEN logic with a DO group to preserve the original values from the master data set. You must rename variables with the RENAME= option because the master and transaction data sets contain the same variables.

Input Data Sets

Both data sets have the same variables.

	MASTER				TRANS		
OBS	ITEMA	ITEMB	ITEMC	OBS	ITEMA	ITEMB	ITEMC
1	1	2	0	1	1	5	6
2	1	3	99	2	3	3	4
3	1	4	88				
4	1	5	77				
5	2	1	66				
6	2	2	55				
7	3	4	44				

Resulting Data Set

Output 3.4   FINAL Data Set

	FINAL		
OBS	ITEMA	ITEMB	ITEMC
1	1	5	6
2	1	5	6
3	1	5	6
4	1	5	6
5	2	1	66
6	2	2	55
7	3	3	4

Program

The objective is to update all variable values in observations from MASTER with the values of variables contained in observations in TRANS, based on the values of the BY variable ITEMA. Because both data sets contain the same variables, you must rename variables other than the BY variable so that variable values from observations in MASTER will not be overlaid.

Special handling is required when TRANS does not contain a matched value for ITEMA in MASTER. Use IF-THEN processing and the IN= option to determine when TRANS contributes to an observation. If TRANS doesn't contribute, then reset the values of ITEMB and ITEMC to their original values from MASTER:

Create FINAL. Combine observations from MASTER and TRANS based on the matching values for the BY variable ITEMA. RENAME= renames the variables ITEMB and ITEMC in MASTER to preserve the values for ITEMB and ITEMC from MASTER. IN= creates the temporary variable IN2, which is set to 1 when an observation from TRANS contributes to the current observation.

```
data final(drop=oldb oldc);
    merge master(rename=(itemb=oldb itemc=oldc)) trans(in=in2);
    by itema;
```

When TRANS does not contribute values for ITEMB and ITEMC based on the current value of ITEMA, use the values from MASTER. If the value of IN2 does not equal 1 (is not true), the values of ITEMB and ITEMC are set to the original values from MASTER.

```
    if not in2 then
    do;
        itemb=oldb;
        itemc=oldc;
    end;
run;
```

Example 3.5

Combining and Collapsing Observations Based on a Common Variable

Goal

Reshape the transaction data set, turning related observations into single ones, and match each *collapsed* observation from the transaction data set with an appropriate observation from the master data set, based on the value of a key variable.

Strategy

Combine data from two SAS data sets based on the key variable. Read the master data set sequentially, while using the KEY= option to directly access observations in an indexed transaction data set. When the transaction data set contains multiple observations for the same key value, you can collapse them into a single observation as you combine it with an observation from the MASTER data set. Use error-checking logic to direct execution to the appropriate code path.

Input Data Sets

SSN is common to both TRANS and MASTER. MASTER contains only unique values of SSN, but TRANS can contain up to three observations with the same value for SSN.

Because the program depends on accessing observations in TRANS directly using KEY=SSN, TRANS must be indexed on the variable SSN. That both data sets be sorted by SSN is not required but is recommended for performance.

	MASTER			TRANS	
OBS	SSN	NAME	OBS	SSN	RECDATE
1	215-15-0007	David	1	202-36-5566	89
2	221-27-1234	Jane	2	215-15-0007	92
3	231-18-1345	Susan	3	215-15-0007	90
4	233-44-3215	Paula	4	215-15-0007	89
5	243-09-8956	Joe	5	221-27-1234	92
			6	221-27-1234	90
			7	221-27-1234	89
			8	231-18-1345	93
			9	231-18-1345	92
			10	243-09-8956	93
			11	243-09-8956	92
			12	243-09-8956	91

Resulting Data Sets

Output 3.5a FINAL1

When All Observations Are Included from MASTER

			FINAL1		
OBS	DATE1	DATE2	DATE3	SSN	NAME
1	92	90	89	215-15-0007	David
2	92	90	89	221-27-1234	Jane
3	93	92	.	231-18-1345	Susan
4	.	.	.	233-44-3215	Paula
5	93	92	91	243-09-8956	Joe

Output 3.5b FINAL2

When Only Matched Observations Are Included from MASTER. See "Related Technique."

```
                              FINAL2

         OBS    DATE1   DATE2   DATE3      SSN        NAME

          1      92      90      89     215-15-0007   David
          2      92      90      89     221-27-1234   Jane
          3      93      92       .     231-18-1345   Susan
          4      93      92      91     243-09-8956   Joe
```

Program

The objective is to combine data from the TRANS data set with the appropriate observations from the MASTER data set. MASTER contains one observation for each value of SSN while TRANS contains multiple observations for some values of SSN. Instead of creating multiple observations in MASTER, this application collapses into a single observation multiple observations from TRANS that contain the same SSN value. This program assumes that TRANS contains no more than three observations with the same value for ID.

First, read one observation from MASTER. Then, by designating SSN as the KEY variable, read all of the observations from TRANS with the same SSN value, and write a single observation to FINAL1. Use an array to assign each RECDATE value from TRANS to DATE1, DATE2, or DATE3, as appropriate. This application assumes that the TRANS data set has been indexed on SSN. It also assumes that no more than three records exist in TRANS for each value of SSN, so the DATEFLD array contains only three elements:

Create FINAL1 and define array DATEFLD. Read an observation from MASTER. In preparation for collapsing multiple observations in TRANS into single observations for each SSN value, the array DATEFLD is defined.

```
data final1(drop=i recdate);
   array datefld(*) date1-date3;
   set master;
```

Reset I to 0 so that each time you process an observation from MASTER, you begin processing the array with the first element. Read an observation from TRANS, based on the value of the key variable SSN. The DO UNTIL loop executes and processes observations from TRANS until all observations with the current value of SSN have been read. (For information on _IORC_ and SYSRC, see the Appendix.)

```
   i=0;
   do until (_iorc_ = %sysrc(_dsenom));
      set trans key=ssn;
```

When an observation from TRANS with
the current value of SSN has been read,
store RECDATE values from TRANS into
an element of the DATEFLD array
(DATE1, DATE2, or DATE3). When the
value of _IORC_ corresponds to _SOK, the
value of SSN in the observation being read
from TRANS matches the current SSN
value from MASTER.

□ *Write an observation to FINAL1 when
all observations from TRANS that have a
matching value for the current value of
SSN from MASTER have been read.* When
the value of _IORC_ corresponds to
_DSENOM, no observations in TRANS
contain the current value of SSN, so the
current observation is written to FINAL1.
ERROR is reset to 0 to prevent an error
condition that would write the contents of
the program data vector to the SAS log.

*In case of an unexpected _IORC_
condition, write an error message and stop
execution.* When _IORC_ corresponds to
anything other than _DSENOM or _SOK,
an unexpected condition has been
encountered, so an error message is written
to the SAS log and the STOP statement
terminates the DATA step.

```
    select(_iorc_);
        when(%sysrc(_sok)) do;
            i + 1;
            datefld(i) = recdate;
        end;




        when(%sysrc(_dsenom)) do;
            output;
            _error_ = 0;
        end;






        otherwise do;
            put 'Unexpected ERROR: _IORC_ = ' _iorc_;
            stop;
        end;
    end;        /* ends SELECT group */
  end;          /* ends DO UNTIL loop */
run;
```

□ Related Technique

*Include all observations from MASTER in
output data set.* See FINAL1 in Output
3.5a.

The program shown previously produces a resulting data set (FINAL1) that
includes all observations in MASTER, due to the logic of the DO group in the
WHEN statement:

```
when(%sysrc(_dsenom)) do;
    output;
    _error_ = 0;
end;
```

To produce a resulting data set (FINAL2) that includes only those observations
from MASTER whose SSN values occur in TRANS, change the statements in
the WHEN statement:

*Include only matching observations in
output data set.* See FINAL2 in Output
3.5b.

```
when(%sysrc(_dsenom)) do;
    if i > 0 then output;
    _error_ = 0;
end;
```

Example 3.6

Applying Transactions to a Master Data Set Using an Index

Goal

Update a master data set in place using values supplied by a transaction data set to locate observations in the master data set that are to be replaced.

Strategy

Overall Strategy

To increase I/O efficiency, read an observation from the transaction data set and keep only the variable that is the key variable in the master data set. Because the master data set can contain multiple occurrences of any value of the key variable, read observations from it until there are no more matches. Each time there is a match, read the current observation from the transaction data set in its entirety and replace the matching observation in the master data set. When no match occurs, you can write a note to the log.

Step-by-Step Strategy

Read the transaction data set sequentially, but use the SET statement with the POINT= option to access observations directly by observation number. Place the SET within an iterative DO loop so that the index variable for the DO loop can supply values to the POINT= variable. Using direct access is important because it makes it possible for you to reread the current observation from the transaction data set when there is a match.

Next, use the MODIFY statement to read an observation from the master data set, retrieving a match based on the values of the KEY= variable. Use the _IORC_ automatic variable and the SYSRC autocall macro in a SELECT group to execute the appropriate statements, based on whether a match is found.

When a match is found, reread the current observation from the transaction data set so that the new values for these variables will overlay the values read from the master data set. Use SET with POINT= to reread the same observation from the transaction data set, this time bringing the values of all variables into the program data vector.

Finally, use the REPLACE statement to update the observation in place in the master data set.

Input Data Sets

Both X and Y are common to the MASTER and TRANS data sets. MASTER contains multiple observations with duplicate values for the key variable X. Because the program depends on directly accessing observations in MASTER by using KEY=X, MASTER must be indexed on the variable X.

MASTER				TRANS		
OBS	X	Y		OBS	X	Y
1	1	2		1	1	8
2	1	3		2	3	9
3	2	4		3	5	2
4	3	5				
5	1	2				

Resulting Data Set

Output 3.6 Updated Version of MASTER Data Set

```
                    MASTER

             OBS    X    Y

              1     1    8
              2     1    8
              3     2    4
              4     3    9
              5     1    8
```

Program

The objective is to update the MASTER data set in place, replacing any observation whose value of the key variable X matches the value of X stored in the TRANS data set. TRANS contains one observation for each value of X, while MASTER contains multiple observations for some values of X.

Use the KEEP= option to read only the variable X from TRANS. Then read an observation from MASTER using the MODIFY statement and the KEY= option. If there is a match for the key variable X in MASTER, reread the same observation from TRANS, this time including all of the variables. These values overlay the existing values in the program data vector that were read from MASTER, and the REPLACE statement updates in place the current observation in MASTER.

To read selected observations from TRANS twice, use the SET statement with the POINT= option to access observations directly by observation number. Use an iterative DO loop to supply values to the POINT= variable for the first SET statement. Then use this same variable (P) as the POINT= variable in the second SET statement, allowing it to read the same observation in TRANS in its entirety. The entire program runs in one iteration of the DATA step.

Use the _IORC_ automatic variable and the SYSRC autocall macro in a SELECT group to route execution to the appropriate code path based on whether a match is found:

Open MASTER for update and execute the iterative DO loop to seqentially process observations from TRANS using direct access by observation number.

```
data master;
   do p = 1 to totobs;
      flag = 0;
      _iorc_ = 0;
      set trans(keep=x) point=p nobs=totobs;

      do while (_iorc_=%sysrc(_sok));
         modify master key=x;
```

Update MASTER in place based on the value of the key variable X. The DO WHILE loop executes and processes observations from MASTER as long as values of X in MASTER match the current value of X in TRANS. (For information on _IORC_ and SYSRC, see the Appendix.)

***When an observation from MASTER
whose key value matches that of TRANS
has been read, reread the current
observation from TRANS and replace the
observation in MASTER.*** When the value
of _IORC_ corresponds to _SOK, the value
of X in the observation being read from
MASTER matches the current X value from
TRANS. The value of the POINT= variable
allows you to reread the current observation
from TRANS, this time reading all of the
variables so their values can overlay the
existing values from MASTER.

***When no match is found, no further
attempts are made to retrieve observations
from MASTER and the DO WHILE loop
ends. An appropriate note is written to the
log indicating that no matches exist for the
current key value.*** When the value of
IORC corresponds to _DSENOM, no
observations in MASTER contain the
current value of X. The _ERROR_
automatic variable is reset to 0 to prevent an
error condition that would write the
contents of the program data vector to the
SAS log. The value of FLAG determines
which note is written to the log.

***In case of an unexpected _IORC_
condition, write an error message to the
SAS log and stop execution.*** When _IORC_
corresponds to anything other than
_DSENOM or _SOK, an unexpected
condition has been encountered, so an error
message is written to the SAS log and the
STOP statement terminates the DATA step.
ERROR is reset to 0 to prevent an error
condition that would write the contents of
the program data vector to the log. The
second STOP statement is necessary to end
the DATA step upon exiting the iterative
DO loop because there is no end-of-file
condition to stop the DATA step when the
SET statement uses POINT=.

```
      select (_iorc_);
         when (%sysrc(_sok)) do;
            set trans point=p;
            flag=1;
            replace;
         end;




         when (%sysrc(_dsenom)) do;
            if flag then
               put 'NOTE: No more matches for KEY = ' x;
            else
               put 'NOTE: No match for KEY = ' x;
            _error_ = 0;
         end;




         otherwise do;
            put 'ERROR: _IORC_ = ' _iorc_ / 'Program halted.';
            _error_ = 0;
            stop;
         end;
      end;          /* ends SELECT group    */
   end;             /* ends DO WHILE loop   */
end;                /* ends iterative DO loop */
stop;
run;
```

Example 3.7

Removing Observations from a Master Data Set Based on Values in a Transaction Data Set

Goal

Update a master data set in place using values supplied by a transaction data set to locate observations in the master data set that are to be deleted.

Strategy

Process observations from the transaction data set sequentially, supplying values to locate observations that are to be deleted in the master data set. Use the MODIFY statement to update a data set in place and the KEY= option to directly access the master data set by using an index on the KEY= variable. Verify the results of the MODIFY execution using the automatic variable _IORC_ and the SYSRC autocall macro. Use the REMOVE statement to delete any match in the master data set. Use an iterative process to access all observations in the master data set that have a match for the current key value. When all observations for the current key value have been deleted or when the master data set does not contain the key value supplied by the transaction data set, continue processing to the next key value from the transaction data set. The task is complete when all observations from the transaction data set have been processed.

You can perform the same task with PROC SQL; see "Related Technique."

Note: Due to the variability of data and the number of conditions that determine the path chosen by the PROC SQL optimizer, it is not always possible to determine the most efficient method without first testing with your data.

Input Data Sets

CUST is common to both TRANS and MASTER, and MASTER contains multiple observations with the same value for CUST. Because the program depends on directly accessing observations in MASTER by using KEY=CUST, MASTER must be indexed on the variable CUST.

	MASTER			TRANS	
OBS	CUST	X		OBS	CUST
1	1	1		1	1
2	1	2		2	3
3	1	3			
4	2	2			
5	2	2			
6	2	2			
7	2	2			
8	3	3			
9	3	3			
10	4	2			

Resulting Data Set

Output 3.7a Updated Version of
MASTER Data Set

MASTER was updated with the DATA
step.

```
                                MASTER

                    OBS      CUST      X

                     4         2       2
                     5         2       2
                     6         2       2
                     7         2       2
                    10         4       2
```

Output 3.7b Updated Version of
MASTER Data Set

MASTER was updated with PROC SQL.

```
                                MASTER

                    OBS      CUST      X

                     4         2       2
                     5         2       2
                     6         2       2
                     7         2       2
                    10         4       2
```

Program

The objective is to update the MASTER data set in place, removing any observation whose value of the key variable CUST matches the value of CUST stored in the TRANS data set. TRANS contains one observation for each value of CUST, while MASTER contains multiple observations for some values of CUST.

Read an observation from TRANS to obtain a value of CUST. Execute the MODIFY statement with the KEY= option to directly access MASTER using the index defined for CUST. To verify whether a match has been located, use the SYSRC autocall macro and the _IORC_ automatic variable. When a match occurs, the REMOVE statement deletes the observation just retrieved and updates MASTER in place. When no match occurs, FLAG is set to prevent further retrievals for the current value of CUST.

To delete multiple observations when MASTER contains duplicates, enclose the MODIFY statement in the DO UNTIL loop to continue execution for the current value of CUST. After all occurrences have been retrieved and deleted, the *no match* condition _DSENOM is encountered, FLAG is set, and the loop terminates. The DATA step iterates and processing continues with the next value of CUST retrieved from TRANS. The DATA step processing terminates when the end-of-file condition is encountered for TRANS:

*Open MASTER for update. Read an
observation from TRANS.*

```
data master;
   set trans;
```

**Remove observations in MASTER based
on the value of the key variable CUST.** The
DO UNTIL loop executes and processes
observations from MASTER until all
observations with the current value of
CUST have been read and deleted. (For
information on _IORC_ and SYSRC, see
the Appendix.)

**When an observation from MASTER has
been read whose key value matches that of
TRANS, remove the observation from
MASTER.** When the value of _IORC_
corresponds to _SOK, the value of CUST in
the observation being read from MASTER
matches the current CUST value from
TRANS.

**When no match is found, no further
observations are retrieved and the
DO UNTIL loop ends.** When the value of
IORC corresponds to _DSENOM, no
observations in MASTER contain the
current value of CUST. _ERROR_ is reset
to 0 to prevent an error condition that would
write the contents of the program data
vector to the SAS log. When the value of
FLAG is 1, the DO UNTIL loop will not
begin a new iteration.

**In case of an unexpected _IORC_
condition, write an error message and stop
execution.** When _IORC_ corresponds to
anything other than _DSENOM or _SOK,
an unexpected condition has been
encountered, so an error message is written
to the SAS log and the STOP statement
terminates the DATA step.

```
flag=0;
do until(flag);
   modify master key=cust;




   select (_iorc_);
      when (%sysrc(_sok)) remove;




      when (%sysrc(_dsenom))
         do;
            _error_=0;
            flag=1;
         end;




      otherwise
         do;
            put 'Unexpected ERROR: _iorc_= ' _iorc_;
            stop;
         end;
   end;        /* ends SELECT group  */
   end;        /* ends DO UNTIL loop */
run;
```

Related Technique

If you are familiar with Structured Query Language (SQL), you may want to use PROC SQL instead of the DATA step. You can use a DELETE statement in PROC SQL to delete rows from a table.* The rows that meet the criteria specified in the WHERE clause are deleted.

```
proc sql;
    delete from master
        where cust in (select cust from trans);
quit;
```

The WHERE clause in this example uses a *subquery*, which is a query that returns one or more values. First, PROC SQL evaluates the subquery and returns all the values for CUST from the TRANS table. The WHERE clause then evaluates to where cust in (1, 3). Thus, all rows in MASTER that have values of 1 or 3 for CUST are deleted.

Note: In PROC SQL, DELETE statements do not automatically produce a report.

Where to Go from Here

☐ **MODIFY with KEY=.** For a discussion of processing using MODIFY with KEY=, see Chapter 1, "SAS Language Statements," in SAS Technical Report P-242 *SAS Software: Changes and Enhancements, Release 6.08.*

---

* A PROC SQL table is a SAS data set. In SQL terminology, columns are variables and rows are observations.

Example 3.8

Performing a Table Lookup with a Small Lookup Data Set

Goal

Combine two data sets by using the value of a specific variable to look up information in a small auxiliary or lookup data set and add it to information in the primary data set to create a new data set.

Strategy

Sequentially process observations in a primary data set while using direct access to read observations in the lookup data set until a match is found. This table lookup technique directly accesses the lookup data based on observation number and avoids reading subsequent observations from the lookup data set once a match has been found. This technique is best used with a small lookup data set because there is the possibility of having to read many records from the lookup data set when trying to find a match.

To read the primary data set, use the SET statement to read one observation on each iteration of the DATA step. To read the lookup data set, use the SET statement with the NOBS= and POINT= options and an iterative DO loop to access each observation by observation number. Then you can test a condition to determine whether combining the information from the current observation of each data set is appropriate and write an observation to a new data set only when the condition is met. Use the RENAME= option to rename the common variable from the lookup data set so that the value read does not overwrite the value read from the primary data set.

You can perform the same task with PROC SQL; see "Related Technique."

Note: Due to the variability of data and the number of conditions that determine the path chosen by the PROC SQL optimizer, it is not always possible to determine the most efficient method without first testing with your data.

Input Data Sets

Both data sets have the common variable PARTNO.

	PRIMARY				LOOKUP	
OBS	PARTNO	QUANTITY		OBS	PARTNO	DESC
1	A220	4		1	A401	tuning peg
2	A498	4		2	A025	bridge
3	A063	8		3	A203	nut
4	A810	4		4	A220	neck
				5	A810	pick guard
				6	A063	pickup
				7	A047	pot
				8	A608	volume knob
				9	A097	toggle switch
				10	A498	body

Resulting Data Sets

Output 3.8a REPORT1 Data Set

REPORT1 was created with the DATA step.

```
                              REPORT1

        OBS      PARTNO     QUANTITY     DESC

         1       A220          4         neck
         2       A498          4         body
         3       A063          8         pickup
         4       A810          4         pick guard
```

Output 3.8b REPORT2 Data Set

REPORT2 was created with PROC SQL.

```
                              REPORT2

        OBS      PARTNO     QUANTITY     DESC

         1       A220          4         neck
         2       A810          4         pick guard
         3       A063          8         pickup
         4       A498          4         body
```

Program

The objective is to create a new data set that includes all of the information from PRIMARY and only the corresponding descriptive information from LOOKUP. The resulting data set, REPORT1, contains the part number, quantity, and description. Read an observation from PRIMARY and subsequently read observations from LOOKUP until a match is found. Use RENAME= to rename PARTNO in LOOKUP so PARTNO values from LOOKUP and PRIMARY are both retained. Use IF-THEN logic to compare the values and to output only matching observations:

Create REPORT1. Read an observation from PRIMARY.

```
data report1(drop=pn found);
   set primary;

   found=0;
   do n=1 to numobs until (found);
      set lookup (rename=(partno=pn)) nobs=numobs point=n;
```

Set FOUND to 0. Read observations from LOOKUP until a match is found based on the value of the common variable, PARTNO. The POINT= option creates a variable (N) whose value provides direct access to each observation in LOOKUP by observation number. NOBS= assigns the number of observations in LOOKUP to the variable NUMOBS. The DO loop iterates once for each observation in LOOKUP or until a match is found. RENAME= renames PARTNO in LOOKUP so the common variable values from LOOKUP do not overwrite the values from PRIMARY. Use IF-THEN logic to compare PARTNO from each data set and output the appropriate values to REPORT1.

Write an observation to REPORT1 if the condition is met. Set FOUND to 1 so the DO loop stops and no more observations are read from LOOKUP until the next observation from PRIMARY is read.

```
        if partno=pn then
           do;
              output;
              found=1;
           end;
     end;

     if not found then put 'No match for PARTNO=' partno 'in LOOKUP.'
        ' Observation not added to REPORT1 data set.';
run;
```

Write a note to the log when there is no match.

Related Technique

If you are familiar with Structured Query Language (SQL), you may want to use PROC SQL instead of the DATA step. PROC SQL joins the tables* to produce a new table, REPORT2. The REPORT2 table is the same as REPORT1, except for the order of the data. The difference in the order is a result of the different processing techniques.

Conceptually, the join results in an internal table that matches every row in PRIMARY with every row in LOOKUP. The WHERE clause determines that only the rows that have matching values for PARTNO will be in the resulting table. The table REPORT2 has the quantity and description for each part that is in both input tables:

```
proc sql;
   create table report2 as
      select *
         from primary, lookup
         where primary.partno=lookup.partno;
quit;
```

Note: In PROC SQL, SELECT *statements* automatically produce a report. SELECT *clauses*, which follow CREATE TABLE or CREATE VIEW statements, do not automatically produce a report.

---

* A PROC SQL table is a SAS data set. In SQL terminology, columns are variables and rows are observations.

Example 3.9

Performing a Table Lookup with Large Nonindexed Data Sets

Goal

Efficiently combine two data sets when one is a large data set whose retrieved values remain fairly constant.

Strategy

Use a table lookup technique that relates data using a user-written format rather than sequentially processing both data sets. Dynamically build the format and retrieve the formatted values. This technique is efficient when you have a large data set whose retrieved values remain fairly constant and when no index is otherwise needed for the data sets.

First, create a data set that you can use to pass information from the lookup file to the FORMAT procedure to dynamically build the format. Specify this data set in the CNTLIN= option as input to the FORMAT procedure. PROC FORMAT uses the data in the input control data set to build the format. Create a new data set by reading observations from the primary file and using the PUT function to apply the formatted values of the common variable to a new variable.

🔍 See "A Closer Look" for more information on dynamically building formats and retrieving values.

You can perform the same task with PROC SQL; see " Related Technique."

Note: Due to the variability of data and the number of conditions that determine the path chosen by the PROC SQL optimizer, it is not always possible to determine the most efficient method without first testing with your data.

Input Data Sets

Both data sets have the common variable PARTNO.

	PRIMARY			LOOKUP	
OBS	PARTNO	QUANTITY	OBS	PARTNO	DESC
1	A220	4	1	A401	tuning peg
2	A498	4	2	A025	bridge
3	A063	8	3	A203	nut
4	A810	4	4	A220	neck
			5	A810	pick guard
			6	A063	pickup
			7	A047	pot
			8	A608	volume knob
			9	A097	toggle switch
			10	A498	body

Resulting Data Set

Output 3.9a REPORT1 Data Set

REPORT1 was created with the DATA
step.

```
                                    REPORT1

                 OBS     PARTNO    QUANTITY    DESC

                  1      A220         4        neck
                  2      A498         4        body
                  3      A063         8        pickup
                  4      A810         4        pick guard
```

Output 3.9b REPORT2 Data Set

REPORT2 was created with PROC SQL.

```
                                    REPORT2

                 OBS     PARTNO    QUANTITY    DESC

                  1      A220         4        neck
                  2      A498         4        body
                  3      A063         8        pickup
                  4      A810         4        pick guard
```

Program

The objective is to create a new data set that includes all of the data from
PRIMARY and only the corresponding descriptive information from
LOOKUP. The resulting data set, REPORT1, contains the part number,
quantity, and description. Create the data set FORMATS, which takes the
information contained in LOOKUP, renaming variables and adding a
FMTNAME variable so that PROC FORMAT can use it to dynamically build
the format $PARTS. Execute PROC FORMAT. Then create REPORT1, which
reads from PRIMARY and applies the formatted values of the key variable
PARTNO from LOOKUP to the new variable DESC:

Create the control data set FORMATS.
Read from LOOKUP and rename the
variables that are required for the
CNTLIN= data set. Rename PARTNO to
START and rename DESC to LABEL.
Assign the required variable FMTNAME
the value $PARTS.

```
data formats;
    set lookup(rename=(partno=start desc=label));
    fmtname='$parts';
run;
```

■ *Use CNTLIN= to build the format*
$PARTS. dynamically.

```
proc format cntlin=formats;
run;
```

Create the data set REPORT1. Read from
PRIMARY and create the new variable
DESC. The PUT function relates the values
of the format $PARTS. to the common
variable PARTNO from LOOKUP, and the
results are stored in the new character
variable DESC.

```
data report1;
    set primary;
    desc=put(partno,$parts.);
run;
```

◪ A Closer Look

Using Formats to Perform a Table Lookup

When you need to perform a table lookup, a common technique is to use a merge operation with the IN= option and the BY statement. However, when you have a large primary data set and a small, unsorted lookup data set, using formats is much more efficient. A user-written format created with PROC FORMAT uses a binary search technique to take the input value and match it with the appropriate output value. The binary search searches half or less of the master file sequentially and does not require that you sort the data. On average, a binary search requires int(log2(*n*)) seek operations to find the desired key value. This solution is preferable as the size of the lookup table increases with respect to the master data set.

Building a format dynamically with CNTLIN=

This example uses FORMATS, a temporary data set, which is specified with the CNTLIN= option as input to the FORMAT procedure. PROC FORMAT uses the contents of this data set to construct formats and informats. A data set specified with CNTLIN= must contain the required variables START, LABEL, and FMTNAME. Once the data set is created with the required variables, you can use CNTLIN= to build formats dynamically (in this example, $PARTS.).

Related Technique

If you are familiar with Structured Query Language (SQL), you may want to use PROC SQL instead of the DATA step. Using the PRIMARY table,[*] PROC SQL creates a new table, REPORT2, that has a new column, DESC. The PUT function assigns values to DESC by using the $PARTS. format, created earlier, with the PARTNO column. The $PARTS. format contains a description for each part represented in the PARTNO column:

```
proc sql;
   create table report2 as
      select *, put(partno,$parts.) as desc
         from primary;
quit;
```

Note: In PROC SQL, SELECT *statements* automatically produce a report. SELECT *clauses*, which follow CREATE TABLE or CREATE VIEW statements, do not automatically produce a report.

---

[*] A PROC SQL table is a SAS data set. In SQL terminology, columns are variables and rows are observations.

Example 3.10

Performing a Table Lookup Using a Composite Index When the Transaction Data Set Contains Duplicate Values

Goal

Combine two data sets by using the value of specific variables to locate information in an auxiliary or *lookup* data set and add it to information from the *primary* data set.

Strategy

Use the iterative action of the DATA step to read the primary file sequentially. Directly access observations in the lookup file by using a composite index. Specify the composite index with the KEY= option on the SET statement and use the UNIQUE option to force each search for a match to begin at the beginning of the index. Because the primary file contains consecutive duplicate values of the variables represented in the composite index, some existing matches might not be found unless each search begins at the beginning of the index. Use the _IORC_ automatic variable and the SYSRC autocall macro in error-checking logic to direct execution to the appropriate code path.

You can perform the same task with PROC SQL; see "Related Technique."

Note: Due to the variability of data and the number of conditions that determine the path chosen by the PROC SQL optimizer, it is not always possible to determine the most efficient method without first testing with your data.

Input Data Sets

STORE and LOC are common to both the PRIMARY and LOOKUP data sets. LOOKUP has a composite index on STORE and LOC. PRIMARY contains duplicate observations with the same values for STORE and LOC.*

PRIMARY

OBS	STORE	LOC	ITEM	AMOUNT
1	1	233	DEBIT	$350
2	1	233	DEBIT	$550
3	1	735	DEBIT	$650
4	1	735	DEBIT	$250
5	1	233	CREDIT	$450
6	1	233	CREDIT	$300
7	2	222	DEBIT	$20
8	2	222	DEBIT	$10
9	2	444	CREDIT	$775
10	2	444	CREDIT	$995
11	2	399	CREDIT	$1,000
12	2	399	CREDIT	$2,500

LOOKUP

OBS	STORE	LOC	STORNAME	CITY
1	1	233	Lynn's Finest	St Thomas
2	1	735	Lynn's Finest	San Diego
3	1	234	Lynn's Finest	Orlando
4	2	222	Just 4 You	San Francisco
5	2	444	Just 4 You	New York
6	2	399	Just 4 You	Boston

---

* For an explanation of the behavior of SET with KEY= when duplicates exist, see SAS Technical Report P-242, *SAS Software: Changes and Enhancements, Release 6.08*, page 14.

Resulting Data Sets

Output 3.10a REPORT1 Data Set

REPORT1 was created with the DATA step.

```
                             REPORT1

    OBS     STORNAME       CITY           ITEM     AMOUNT

     1    Lynn's Finest   St Thomas      DEBIT      $350
     2    Lynn's Finest   St Thomas      DEBIT      $550
     3    Lynn's Finest   San Diego      DEBIT      $650
     4    Lynn's Finest   San Diego      DEBIT      $250
     5    Lynn's Finest   St Thomas      CREDIT     $450
     6    Lynn's Finest   St Thomas      CREDIT     $300
     7    Just 4 You      San Francisco  DEBIT       $20
     8    Just 4 You      San Francisco  DEBIT       $10
     9    Just 4 You      New York       CREDIT     $775
    10    Just 4 You      New York       CREDIT     $995
    11    Just 4 You      Boston         CREDIT   $1,000
    12    Just 4 You      Boston         CREDIT   $2,500
```

Output 3.10b REPORT2 Data Set

REPORT2 was created with PROC SQL.

```
                             REPORT2

    OBS     STORNAME       CITY           ITEM     AMOUNT

     1    Lynn's Finest   St Thomas      DEBIT      $350
     2    Lynn's Finest   St Thomas      DEBIT      $550
     3    Lynn's Finest   San Diego      DEBIT      $650
     4    Lynn's Finest   San Diego      DEBIT      $250
     5    Lynn's Finest   St Thomas      CREDIT     $450
     6    Lynn's Finest   St Thomas      CREDIT     $300
     7    Just 4 You      San Francisco  DEBIT       $20
     8    Just 4 You      San Francisco  DEBIT       $10
     9    Just 4 You      New York       CREDIT     $775
    10    Just 4 You      New York       CREDIT     $995
    11    Just 4 You      Boston         CREDIT   $1,000
    12    Just 4 You      Boston         CREDIT   $2,500
```

Program

The objective is to create a new data set that includes information from PRIMARY and the corresponding descriptive information from LOOKUP. The resulting data set, REPORT1, contains the store name, city, item, and amount. Read an observation from PRIMARY using sequential access. Using the composite index STORLOC, read an observation from LOOKUP directly based on the current values of variables STORE and LOC. Because PRIMARY contains duplicate values, you must begin each search on the STORLOC index for the LOOKUP data set at the beginning. Otherwise, you would miss matches in LOOKUP for consecutive duplicate values of STORLOC in PRIMARY.

Create REPORT1. Read an observation from PRIMARY.

```
data report1(drop=store loc);
   set primary;
```

Read from LOOKUP with direct access, based on values in the composite index STORLOC. UNIQUE causes the search to always begin at the beginning of the index, so that consecutive duplicate values in PRIMARY will not miss a match in LOOKUP.

```
   set lookup key=storloc/unique;
```

When the current values of STORE and LOC from PRIMARY match a STORLOC index value from LOOKUP, write an observation to REPORT1. When the value of _IORC_ corresponds to _SOK, there is a match.

```
   select (_iorc_);
      when (%sysrc(_SOK)) output;
```

When the current values of STORE and LOC from PRIMARY do not match a STORLOC index value from LOOKUP, write a warning message to the log. When the value of _IORC_ corresponds to _DSENOM, there is no match. The PUT statement writes a message to the log. Setting _ERROR_ to 0 prevents the error condition from writing the entire contents of the program data vector to the log.

```
      when (%sysrc(_dsenom))
         do;
            put 'WARNING!  New Location not in Table' store= loc=;
            _error_=0;
         end;
```

In case of an unexpected _IORC_ condition, write an error message to the SAS log and stop execution. When _IORC_ corresponds to anything other than _DSENOM or _SOK, an unexpected condition has been encountered, so an error message is written to the SAS log and the STOP statement terminates the DATA step. _ERROR_ is reset to 0 to prevent an error condition that would write the contents of the program data vector to the log.

```
      otherwise
         do;
            put 'Unexpected ERROR:  _IORC_ =  ' _iorc_;
            _error_=0;
            stop;
         end;
   end;
run;
```

Related Technique

If you are familiar with Structured Query Language (SQL), you may want to use PROC SQL instead of the DATA step. PROC SQL joins the tables[*] to produce a new table, REPORT2. The REPORT2 table is the same as REPORT1.

Conceptually, the join results in an internal table that matches every row in PRIMARY with every row in LOOKUP. However, you want only the rows where the values for STORE and LOC are the same. The WHERE clause returns the rows from the join that have the same values for STORE and LOC. Thus, the result is a table that includes information from both tables, based on the columns they have in common:

```
proc sql;
   create table report2 as
      select storname, city, item, amount
         from  primary p, lookup l
         where p.store=l.store and p.loc=l.loc;
quit;
```

Note: In PROC SQL, SELECT *statements* automatically produce a report. SELECT *clauses*, which follow CREATE TABLE or CREATE VIEW statements, do not automatically produce a report.

---

[*] A PROC SQL table is a SAS data set. In SQL terminology, columns are variables and rows are observations.

Example 3.11

Performing a Table Lookup with a Large Lookup Data Set That Is Indexed

Goal

Efficiently combine two data sets when the lookup data set is large and has an index.

Strategy

Use a table lookup technique that is especially appropriate for a large lookup data set. Perform a table lookup using an index to locate observations that have key values equal to the current value of the *key variable*. Read from the primary file sequentially. Then to read the lookup data set, use the SET statement with the KEY= option to access the observations directly. Observations are written to the output data set only when a match occurs in the lookup data set for the key value supplied by the primary data set. Use error-checking logic to direct execution to the appropriate code path.

You can perform the same task with PROC SQL, see "Related Technique."

Note: Due to the variability of data and the number of conditions that determine the path chosen by the PROC SQL optimizer, it is not always possible to determine the most efficient method without first testing with your data.

Input Data Sets

PARTNO is common to both the PRIMARY and LOOKUP data sets. PRIMARY contains no consecutive duplicate values for PARTNO.* Because the program depends on directly accessing observations in LOOKUP by using KEY=PARTNO, LOOKUP must be indexed on the variable PARTNO.

	PRIMARY			LOOKUP	
OBS	PARTNO	QUANTITY	OBS	PARTNO	DESC
1	A063	8	1	A401	tuning peg
2	A220	4	2	A025	bridge
3	A498	4	3	A203	nut
4	A777	3	4	A220	neck
5	A810	4	5	A810	pick guard
			6	A063	pickup
			7	A047	pot
			8	A608	volume knob
			9	A097	toggle switch
			10	A498	body

---

*   This program works as expected only if PRIMARY contains no consecutive observations with the same value for PARTNO. For an explanation of the behavior of SET with KEY= when duplicates exist, see SAS Technical Report P-242, *SAS Software: Changes and Enhancements, Release 6.08*, page 14.

Resulting Data Sets

Output 3.11a   REPORT1 Data Set

REPORT1 was created with the DATA step.

```
                                 REPORT1

              OBS     PARTNO    QUANTITY    DESC

               1      A063         8        pickup
               2      A220         4        neck
               3      A498         4        body
               4      A810         4        pick guard
```

Output 3.11b   REPORT2 Data Set

REPORT2 was created with PROC SQL.

```
                                 REPORT2

              OBS     PARTNO    QUANTITY    DESC

               1      A063         8        pickup
               2      A220         4        neck
               3      A498         4        body
               4      A810         4        pick guard
```

Program

The objective is to create a new data set that includes all of the information from PRIMARY and only the corresponding descriptive information from LOOKUP. The resulting data set, REPORT1, contains the part number, quantity, and description.

First, read an observation from PRIMARY. Then, use the SET statement with the KEY= option to read an observation from LOOKUP based on the current value of PARTNO. To verify whether a matching value in LOOKUP has been located for the current value of PARTNO in PRIMARY, use the SYSRC autocall macro and the _IORC_ automatic variable. When a match is found, write the observation. When no match is found, write a warning message to the SAS log, reset _ERROR_ to 0, and continue processing. When an unexpected condition is encountered, write an error message and stop execution:

Create REPORT1. Read an observation from PRIMARY.

```
data report1;
   set primary;
```

Read an observation from LOOKUP based on the value of the key variable, PARTNO. The SET statement with KEY= accesses an observation in LOOKUP directly through the index, using the current value of PARTNO.

```
   set lookup key=partno;
```

When an observation from LOOKUP has been successfully located and retrieved, write it to REPORT1. When the value of _IORC_ corresponds to _SOK, the value of PARTNO in the observation being read from LOOKUP matches the current PARTNO value from PRIMARY. (For information on _IORC_ and SYSRC, see the Appendix.)

```
   select (_iorc_);
      when (%sysrc(_SOK)) output;
```

When no match is found, write a warning message to the SAS log. When the value of _IORC_ corresponds to _DSENOM, no observations in LOOKUP contain the current value of PARTNO. _ERROR_ is reset to 0 to prevent an error condition that would write the contents of the program data vector to the SAS log.

```
      when (%sysrc(_dsenom))
         do;
             put 'WARNING:  Part number ' partno 'is not in lookup table.';
             _error_=0;
         end;
```

In case of an unexpected _IORC_ condition, write an error message to the SAS log and stop execution. When _IORC_ corresponds to anything other than _DSENOM or _SOK, an unexpected condition has been encountered, so an error message is written to the SAS log and the STOP statement terminates the DATA step.

```
      otherwise do;
         put 'Unexpected ERROR:  _IORC_ = ' _iorc_;
         stop;
      end;
    end;
  run;
```

Related Technique

If you are familiar with Structured Query Language (SQL), you may want to use PROC SQL instead of the DATA step. PROC SQL joins the tables[*] to produce a new table, REPORT2. The REPORT2 table is the same as REPORT1, except for the order of the data. The difference in order is a result of the join method chosen by the internal optimizer.

Conceptually, a join results in an internal table that matches every row in PRIMARY with every row in LOOKUP. The WHERE clause determines that the join will return only the rows that have matching values for PARTNO. The table REPORT2 has the quantity and description for each part that is in both input tables:

```
proc sql;
   create table report2 as
      select *
         from primary, lookup
         where primary.partno=lookup.partno;
quit;
```

Note: In PROC SQL, SELECT *statements* automatically produce a report. SELECT *clauses*, which follow CREATE TABLE or CREATE VIEW statements, do not automatically produce a report.

---

[*] A PROC SQL table is a SAS data set. In SQL terminology, columns are variables and rows are observations.

CHAPTER 4

Combining Multiple Observations with Multiple Observations

The many-to-many category implies that multiple observations from each input data set may be related based on the values of a common variable.

Example 4.1

Adding Variables from a Transaction Data Set to a Master Data Set

Goal

Based on the values of a common variable, produce a new data set by combining variables from a master data set and a transaction data set. Include only observations that the master data set contains.

Strategy

Use the MERGE statement with the BY statement to combine the observations from the two data sets. Use the IN= data set option to indicate whether the master data set contributed to an observation. To get the desired results, set the value of the temporary variable created with IN= to 0 at the top of the DATA step to reset the value when the BY variable changes. While merging observations within each BY group, use the subsetting IF statement to allow the DATA step to complete the current iteration and to write an observation only when the master data set has contributed to it.

This *match-merge* operation requires that each data set either have an index on the BY variable or be sorted by the values of the BY variable.

Input Data Sets

Both the master and transaction data sets may contain duplicate values for the BY variable NAME.

	MASTER				TRANS	
OBS	NAME	Y		OBS	NAME	Z
1	John	1111		1	John	89
2	John	2222		2	John	94
3	John	3333		3	John	83
4	Mary	1111		4	Mary	77
				5	Mary	88
				6	Mary	99

Resulting Data Set

Output 4.1a COMBINED Data Set

	COMBINED		
OBS	NAME	Y	Z
1	John	1111	89
2	John	2222	94
3	John	3333	83
4	Mary	1111	77

Output 4.1b COMBINE2 Data Set

COMBINE2 contains two additional
observations for MARY that did not exist in
MASTER. See "Related Technique."

	COMBINE2		
OBS	NAME	Y	Z
1	John	1111	89
2	John	2222	94
3	John	3333	83
4	Mary	1111	77
5	Mary	1111	88
6	Mary	1111	99

Program

The objective is to combine observations from MASTER and TRANS based
on the values of a common variable, including only those observations to
which MASTER contributes. Use the MERGE and BY statements to combine
observations from the two data sets. Use the subsetting IF statement and the
IN= data set option to determine when MASTER has contributed variables.
Reset the IN= variable to 0 at the top of the DATA step. Otherwise this value,
which is retained until the BY group changes, may cause the DATA step to
write additional observations to COMBINED from TRANS.

*Create COMBINED. Combine
observations from MASTER and TRANS
based on the matching values for the BY
variable NAME.* IN= creates INMAST,
which is set to 1 when an observation from
MASTER contributes to the current
observation. INMAST is set to 0 at the top
of the DATA step so that a previous value
of 1 is not retained until the BY group
changes.

*Allow the DATA step to complete the
current iteration and write an observation
to COMBINED only if MASTER has
contributed to it.*

```
data combined;
   inmast=0;
   merge master(in=inmast) trans;
   by name;




   if inmast;
run;
```

Related Technique

The preceding program writes an observation to COMBINED only if the
MASTER data set contributed. In the input data sets, TRANS contains three
observations with the value of MARY for NAME, but MASTER contains only
one. If in your application you want the resulting output data set to contain
multiple observations when the transaction data set does but the master data set
does not, then simply remove the assignment statement that sets the value of
the IN= variable to 0. In this example, if you do not reset INMAST to 0, its
value is retained throughout the BY group. Three observations, therefore,
containing the value MARY for NAME are created and written to the output
data set COMBINE2. See Output 4.1b.

```
data combine2;
   merge master(in=inmast) trans;
   by name;
   if inmast;
run;
```

Example 4.2

Updating a Master Data Set with Only Nonmissing Values from a Transaction Data Set

---

Goal

Update a master data set with values from a transaction data set, except when the transaction data set contains missing values for the variable being updated.

Strategy

Use the MERGE statement with the BY statement to update values in a master data set with values from a transaction data set. Use IF-THEN logic in conjunction with the RENAME= data set option to apply transaction values only if they are not missing values.

This *match-merge* operation requires that each data set either have an index on the BY variable or be sorted by the values of the BY variable.

Input Data Sets

Both MASTER and TRANS contain duplicate values for the BY variable ITEM. The data sets are sorted by the values of ITEM.

	MASTER				TRANS	
OBS	ITEM	PRICE		OBS	ITEM	PRICE
1	apple	$1.99		1	banana	$1.05
2	apple	$2.89		2	grapes	$2.75
3	apple	$1.49		3	orange	$1.49
4	grapes	$1.69		4	orange	.
5	grapes	$2.46		5	orange	$2.39
6	orange	$2.29				
7	orange	$1.89				
8	orange	$2.19				

Resulting Data Set

Output 4.2 COMBINE Data Set

	COMBINE	
OBS	ITEM	PRICE
1	apple	$1.99
2	apple	$2.89
3	apple	$1.49
4	banana	$1.05
5	grapes	$2.75
6	grapes	$2.75
7	orange	$1.49
8	orange	$1.89
9	orange	$2.39

Program

The objective is to update the observations in MASTER whose ITEM values have a match in TRANS, *except* when the value of the PRICE, the variable being updated, has a missing value in TRANS. The variable PRICE in TRANS is renamed NEWPRICE so that in the program data vector its value does not automatically overlay the value of PRICE read from MASTER. When the value of NEWPRICE is not missing in TRANS, use IF-THEN processing to assign its value to the PRICE variable in MASTER. Otherwise, use the existing value of PRICE in MASTER:

Create COMBINE. Combine observations from MASTER and TRANS based on the matching values for ITEM. RENAME= renames the variable PRICE in TRANS for later processing with the IF-THEN statement.

```
data combine(drop=newprice);
   merge master trans(rename=(price=newprice));
   by item;
```

When NEWPRICE is not equal to missing, use its value to update the MASTER value of PRICE based on the current value of ITEM. If the value of NEWPRICE is missing, PRICE retains its original value from MASTER.

```
   if newprice ne . then price=newprice;
   format price dollar5.2;
run;
```

Example 4.3

Generating Every Combination of Observations (Cartesian Product) between Data Sets

Goal

Combine two tables* that have no common columns in order to produce every possible combination of rows.

Strategy

Join the two tables with PROC SQL. When you join two tables without specifying join criteria in a WHERE clause, you get a Cartesian product. A *Cartesian product* shows every possible combination of rows from the tables being joined. PROC SQL joins the tables listed in the FROM clause.

Input Data Sets

	TRIPS			ATTENDS	
OBS	DEST	TRAVCODE	OBS	NAME	LEVEL
1	DETROIT	C751	1	Kreuger, John	1
2	SAN FRANCISCO	C288	2	Angler, Erica	2
3	ST THOMAS	A054	3	Ng, Sebastian	1
4	HAWAII	P003	4	Sook, Joy	3
5	BERMUDA	A059	5	Silverton, Lou	2

---

* A PROC SQL table is a SAS data set. In SQL terminology, columns are variables and rows are observations.

Resulting Data Set

Output 4.3 FLIGHTS Table

```
                                      FLIGHTS

          OBS      DEST            TRAVCODE    NAME              LEVEL

           1    DETROIT             C751    Kreuger, John         1
           2    DETROIT             C751    Angler, Erica         2
           3    DETROIT             C751    Ng, Sebastian         1
           4    DETROIT             C751    Sook, Joy             3
           5    DETROIT             C751    Silverton, Lou        2
           6    SAN FRANCISCO       C288    Kreuger, John         1
           7    SAN FRANCISCO       C288    Angler, Erica         2
           8    SAN FRANCISCO       C288    Ng, Sebastian         1
           9    SAN FRANCISCO       C288    Sook, Joy             3
          10    SAN FRANCISCO       C288    Silverton, Lou        2
          11    ST THOMAS           A054    Kreuger, John         1
          12    ST THOMAS           A054    Angler, Erica         2
          13    ST THOMAS           A054    Ng, Sebastian         1
          14    ST THOMAS           A054    Sook, Joy             3
          15    ST THOMAS           A054    Silverton, Lou        2
          16    HAWAII              P003    Kreuger, John         1
          17    HAWAII              P003    Angler, Erica         2
          18    HAWAII              P003    Ng, Sebastian         1
          19    HAWAII              P003    Sook, Joy             3
          20    HAWAII              P003    Silverton, Lou        2
          21    BERMUDA             A059    Kreuger, John         1
          22    BERMUDA             A059    Angler, Erica         2
          23    BERMUDA             A059    Ng, Sebastian         1
          24    BERMUDA             A059    Sook, Joy             3
          25    BERMUDA             A059    Silverton, Lou        2
```

Program

Invoke PROC SQL and create a table. The CREATE TABLE statement creates the table FLIGHTS to store the results of the subsequent query.

Select the columns. The SELECT clause selects all of the columns from the tables specified in the FROM clause.

Name the tables to join and query.

Because each flight attendant in ATTENDS flies to each destination, the objective is to produce a table that shows every possible combination of NAME and DEST:

```
proc sql;
   create table flights as



      select *



          from trips, attends;
quit;
```

Note: In PROC SQL, SELECT *statements* automatically produce a report. SELECT *clauses*, which follow CREATE TABLE or CREATE VIEW statements, do not automatically produce a report.

Example 4.4

Generating Every Combination of Observations between Data Sets Based on a Common Variable

Goal

Combine two tables* that have a common column. The common column has duplicate values in both tables. Produce a table that shows the possible combination of rows where the values from the common column match.

Strategy

Join the two tables with PROC SQL. The join produces all possible combinations of rows from both tables. Use a WHERE clause to choose only those rows where the values from the common column match. Order the query result to make the data easier to process in subsequent steps. You do not have to sort the data prior to joining the table.

This technique of showing the possible combinations of observations is useful for producing a table that can be manipulated further.

Input Data Sets

	ROSTER				SCHEDULE		
OBS	GRADE	STUDENT		OBS	GRADE	HOMEROOM	LOCATION
1	11	Jon		1	11	6	room4
2	9	Rick		2	10	3	room1
3	10	Amber		3	12	8	library
4	12	Susan		4	10	4	room2
5	10	Cindy		5	11	5	room3
6	11	Ginny		6	10	2	cafe
7	10	Denise		7	11	7	shop
8	12	Lynn		8	9	1	gym
9	11	Michael					
10	12	Jake					

---

* A PROC SQL table is a SAS data set. In SQL terminology, columns are variables and rows are observations.

Resulting Data Set

Output 4.4 ASSIGN Table

```
                              ASSIGN

       OBS    STUDENT    GRADE    HOMEROOM    LOCATION

        1     Amber       10         2        cafe
        2     Amber       10         4        room2
        3     Amber       10         3        room1
        4     Cindy       10         4        room2
        5     Cindy       10         3        room1
        6     Cindy       10         2        cafe
        7     Denise      10         4        room2
        8     Denise      10         2        cafe
        9     Denise      10         3        room1
       10     Ginny       11         5        room3
       11     Ginny       11         6        room4
       12     Ginny       11         7        shop
       13     Jake        12         8        library
       14     Jon         11         6        room4
       15     Jon         11         5        room3
       16     Jon         11         7        shop
       17     Lynn        12         8        library
       18     Michael     11         5        room3
       19     Michael     11         6        room4
       20     Michael     11         7        shop
       21     Rick         9         1        gym
       22     Susan       12         8        library
```

Program

The objective is to produce a table that shows all of the possible homeroom locations for each student, based on grade.

Join the two tables to find all of the possible combinations of STUDENT and LOCATION. Use the GRADE column to join the tables.* Choose only those rows where the values for GRADE match. Order the data by STUDENT:

Invoke PROC SQL and create a table. The CREATE TABLE statement creates the table ASSIGN to store the results of the subsequent query.

```
proc sql;
   create table assign as
```

Select the columns. The SELECT clause selects the specified columns from the tables specified in the FROM clause. Because GRADE is in both tables, you need to qualify the name by prefixing the table name to the column name.

```
      select student, roster.grade, homeroom, location
```

Name the tables to join and query.

```
      from roster, schedule
```

Specify the join criterion.

```
      where roster.grade=schedule.grade
```

Order the resulting rows by the students' names.

```
      order by student;
quit;
```

Note: In PROC SQL, SELECT *statements* automatically produce a report. SELECT *clauses*, which follow CREATE TABLE or CREATE VIEW statements, do not automatically produce a report.

---

*   The columns that you join on do not have to have the same name.

Example 4.5

Delaying Final Disposition of Observations Until All Processing Is Complete

Goal

Search through a data set multiple times to find the closest match based on calculated criteria, not on matching values of common variables. Flag observations for subsequent processing based on those criteria.

Strategy

Flag observations in a data set for further processing by reading one data set sequentially and another data set directly using the POINT= option. Set up an array with one element for each observation in the second data set, the one you read directly.

Read an observation from the first data set, then begin reading observations from the second data set, looking for values of one or more variables that meet a certain condition set by a value from the observation in the first data set. Use the iterative DO loop and the POINT= option to read all observations not marked as already used from the second data set. Continue reading observations and comparing values to see if a better match occurs in the second data set.

After the entire second data set has been processed to locate the best match for the current observation in the first data set, write an observation that contains the best match to the output data set. Mark the selected observation from the second data set as *used*.

After all observations from the first data set have been processed, write to another output data set all observations from the second data set that were not paired with observations from the first data set.

Input Data Sets

ROOMS indicates that the seating capacity and availability of demo facilities for six currently unscheduled meeting rooms.

ROOMS

OBS	ROOM	DEMOFAC	CAPACITY
1	R100	N	10
2	R200	Y	15
3	R301	Y	30
4	R305	N	50
5	R400	Y	60
6	R420	Y	100

MEETINGS contains one observation for each meeting that needs to be scheduled, the number expected to attend, and whether demo facilities are needed.

MEETINGS

OBS	NUMATT	DEMO	DESC
1	10	Y	Operator Training
2	12	N	Sales Meeting
3	40	Y	Marketing Presentation
4	60	N	Division Meeting
5	45	N	Employee Orientation

Resulting Data Sets

Output 4.5a ASSIGN Data Set

ASSIGN lists the meetings and their assigned rooms. No room was found for the last meeting.

```
                                   ASSIGN

  OBS    NUMATT    DEMO    DESC                    ROOM    DEMOFAC    CAPACITY

   1       10       Y      Operator Training       R200       Y          15
   2       12       N      Sales Meeting           R305       N          50
   3       40       Y      Marketing Presentation  R400       Y          60
   4       60       N      Division Meeting        R420       Y         100
   5       45       N      Employee Orientation    NONE                   .
```

Output 4.5b ROOMS Data Set

ROOMS contains only the rooms that remain unassigned.

```
                         ROOMS

          OBS    ROOM    DEMOFAC    CAPACITY

           1     R100       N          10
           2     R301       Y          30
```

Program

The objective is to find the most suitable room for a meeting, based on the number of attendees and the need for demo facilities. After the first suitable match is found in ROOMS for an observation in MEETING, the rest of the observations in ROOMS are searched in case there is an even more appropriate match. "More appropriate" means that the room is closer in size to the number of attendees or that demo facilities are not scheduled unless they are needed. In this application, keeping demo facilities available was the highest priority.

First, determine the number of observations in ROOMS by using the NOBS= option and write that number to a macro variable using CALL SYMPUT. In the second DATA step, use sequential access to read an observation from MEETINGS. Use the value of the macro variable to create an array with one element for each observation in ROOMS. Create an iterative DO loop that iterates once for each observation in ROOMS. When a room has been scheduled for a meeting, the value of the appropriate element in the array indicates that the room is currently scheduled. If a room is not already tagged as scheduled, read an observation from ROOMS directly using the POINT= option. Determine if the room is large enough; if it has demo facilities, determine if the meeting requires them. Continue reading other observations from ROOMS, testing to see if a more appropriate room is available. Set up temporary variables to hold values for seating capacity and availability of demo facilities so that you can compare those values to ones read from the next observation as you search for an even more suitable room.

At the end of each DATA step iteration, write an observation to ASSIGN. If a match was found, set the USED array element for the appropriate observation from ROOMS to 1. If it wasn't, write the observation and indicate that no room was assigned.

After processing all observations in MEETINGS, reread ROOMS with direct access using SET with POINT= in a DO loop. Write observations to the new version of ROOMS only for those rooms that remain unassigned.

Determine the number of observations in ROOMS and store that value in macro variable NUM. No observations are actually read from MASTER because 0 is never true. MASTER is opened so that the number of observations can be captured from the data set descriptor information. By using CALL SYMPUT to store this number in a macro variable, you can pass it to the next DATA step.

```
data _null_;
   if 0 then set rooms nobs=nobs;
   call symput('num',left(put(nobs,8.)));
   stop;
run;
```

Create ASSIGN and a new version of ROOMS. Define the array USED. Retain the values of the elements in the array across iterations and initialize their values to 0. The macro variable NUM is equal to 6, the number of observations in MASTER. So USED1–USED6 are created to contain a value that indicates whether an observation is flagged as already matched.

```
data rooms(keep = room demofac capacity)
     assign(keep = desc room numatt demo demofac capacity);
   array used(*) used1-used&num;
   retain used1-used&num 0;
```

Read an observation from MEETINGS. Create a variable (DONE) that will equal 1 when the last observation is being processed. After the last observation has been read, conditional processing can execute statements that create another data set containing unassigned rooms.

```
   set meetings end=done;
```

Initialize temporary variables that will be used to store values of CAP, DEMO, and OBS so that values can be compared between observations from ROOMS.

```
   tempcap = 999;
   tempdemo = demo;
   tempobs = .;
```

Begin a DO loop that will read each observation from ROOMS that is not already flagged as used. This DO loop allows the program to scan the entire ROOMS data set in an attempt to find the best unassigned match for each observation in MEETINGS. USED is true (equals 1) when an observation has been designated as already assigned to a meeting. Because POINT= is used, ROOMS is read with direct access instead of sequential. If ROOMS were processed sequentially here, reaching the end of it would end the DATA step, and we would not be able to reread it multiple times.

```
   do i=1 to nobs;
      if used(i) ne 1 then
         do;
            set rooms point=i nobs=nobs;
```

Determine if the current room is large enough and if it has demo facilities if they are necessary. CAPACITY and DEMOFAC are variables from ROOMS that contain information about the meeting room in each observation. NUMATT and DEMO are variables from MEETINGS that show how many people the room must accommodate and if demo equipment is needed.

```
            if capacity >= numatt and (demofac=demo or demo = 'N') then
               do;
```

Determine if the current room is a better fit than the previous choice. If the CAPACITY value of the current room is smaller than that of the previous choice (TEMPCAP) and if the status of demo facility is the same or not needed, then the current room is a better choice. TEMPOBS is set to the value of I, the number of the current observation. It will be used later to set the appropriate member of the USED array to indicate that the room has been selected.

If an exact match is found, leave the iterative DO loop because there is no need to search further.

If a room (from ROOMS) has been found for the current meeting (from MEETINGS), then use the value of TEMPOBS to locate the appropriate observation from ROOMS and reread it. Write the current observation (containing information from MEETINGS and ROOMS) to ASSIGN. Set the value of the USED array element that corresponds to the current observation from ROOMS to 1.

If no room was selected, reset the values of ROOM, CAPACITY, and DEMOFAC appropriately, and write the observation to ASSIGN, indicating that no appropriate room was available.

After all observations in MEETINGS have been processed to locate the best available meeting room in ROOMS, use direct access to read each observation in ROOMS. Write to the new version of the ROOMS data set only those observations that are not flagged as used. The DIM function returns the number of elements in an array. Using DIM prevents you from having to change the upper bound of an iterative DO group if you later change the number of array elements.

```
            if (capacity < tempcap) or
               (demo = 'N' and tempdemo = 'Y') then
               do;
                   tempcap = capacity;
                   tempdemo = demofac;
                   tempobs = i;
               end;
          end;      /* ends a DO group           */



             if tempcap=numatt and tempdemo=demo then leave;
         end;            /* ends a DO group        */
     end;               /* ends an iterative DO loop */

   if tempobs ne . then
      do;
         set rooms point=tempobs;
         output assign;
         used(tempobs)=1;
      end;




   else
      do;
         room = 'NONE';
         capacity = .;
         demofac = ' ';
         output assign;
      end;

   if done then
      do i=1 to dim(used);
         if not used(i) then
            do;
               set rooms point=i;
               output rooms;
            end;
      end;
run;
```

Where to Go from Here

□   **LEAVE statement.** For a complete description with an example, see pp. 34–35 in *SAS Technical Report P-222, Changes and Enhancements to Base SAS Software, Release 6.07.*

Example 4.6

Generating Every Combination between Data Sets, Based on a Common Variable When an Index Is Available

Goal

Create a new data set that is a cartesian product* of two input data sets.

Strategy

The overall strategy is to process the first data set sequentially using BY-group processing and to process the second data set directly based on the value of a key variable. (The variable common to both data sets is the BY variable for the first data set and the key variable for the second data set.) Each time you find a match, write an observation to the output data set. If there are consecutive duplicate values for the common variable in the first data set, you must force the pointer to return to the beginning of the index so that matching values in the second data set will be retrieved and paired with the appropriate observations in the first data set.

In detail, sort the first data set on the BY variable and index the second data set on the same variable. Read observations from the first data set sequentially, executing the SET statement in each iteration of the DATA step. Read an observation from the second data set using SET with the KEY= option in a DO UNTIL loop. Continue reading observations until there is no match for the common variable.

Use the SELECT group to conditionally execute statements based on whether a match is found. If a match is found, write an observation to the output data set. If a match is not found, take different actions, based on whether the current observation from the first data set is the last one in the current BY group. When it is the last in the BY group, take no additional action. The DO UNTIL loop will end.

When the current observation from the first data set is not the last in the current BY group, you must force positioning on the index to the beginning. Otherwise, consecutive duplicate values for the common variable in the first data set cannot be paired with matching values in the second data set.

You can perform the same task with PROC SQL. See "Related Technique."

Note: Due to the variability of data and the number of conditions that determine the path chosen by the PROC SQL optimizer, it is not always possible to determine the most efficient method without first testing with your data.

---

*   In this example, a *Cartesian product* is a new data set that consists of every possible combination of observations from the two input data sets, based on the value of a BY variable.

Input Data Sets

The SALES data set is sorted by PRODUCT.

```
                          SALES

        OBS   PRODUCT   SALESREP   ORDERNUM

         1      310     Polanski   RAL5447
         2      310     Alvarez    CH1443
         3      312     Corrigan   DUR5523
         4      313     Corrigan   DUR5524
         5      313     Polanski   RAL5498
```

The STOCK data set is indexed by PRODUCT.

```
                            STOCK

     OBS   PRODUCT      PRDTDESC        PIECE     PCDESC

      1      310     oak pedestal table  310.01   tabletop
      2      310     oak pedestal table  310.02   pedestal
      3      310     oak pedestal table  310.03   2 leaves
      4      312     brass floor lamp    312.01   lamp base
      5      312     brass floor lamp    312.02   lamp shade
      6      313     oak bookcase, short 313.01   bookcase
      7      313     oak bookcase, short 313.02   2 shelves
```

Resulting Data Set

Output 4.6a SHIPLIST Data Set

SHIPLIST was created with the DATA step.

```
                                 SHIPLIST

   OBS  PRODUCT  SALESREP  ORDERNUM      PRDTDESC         PIECE    PCDESC

    1     310    Polanski  RAL5447   oak pedestal table   310.01  tabletop
    2     310    Polanski  RAL5447   oak pedestal table   310.02  pedestal
    3     310    Polanski  RAL5447   oak pedestal table   310.03  2 leaves
    4     310    Alvarez   CH1443    oak pedestal table   310.01  tabletop
    5     310    Alvarez   CH1443    oak pedestal table   310.02  pedestal
    6     310    Alvarez   CH1443    oak pedestal table   310.03  2 leaves
    7     312    Corrigan  DUR5523   brass floor lamp     312.01  lamp base
    8     312    Corrigan  DUR5523   brass floor lamp     312.02  lamp shade
    9     313    Corrigan  DUR5524   oak bookcase, short  313.01  bookcase
   10     313    Corrigan  DUR5524   oak bookcase, short  313.02  2 shelves
   11     313    Polanski  RAL5498   oak bookcase, short  313.01  bookcase
   12     313    Polanski  RAL5498   oak bookcase, short  313.02  2 shelves
```

Output 4.6b SHIPLST Data Set

SHIPLST was created with PROC SQL.

```
                                 SHIPLST

   OBS  PRODUCT  SALESREP  ORDERNUM      PRDTDESC         PIECE    PCDESC

    1     310    Polanski  RAL5447   oak pedestal table   310.01  tabletop
    2     310    Alvarez   CH1443    oak pedestal table   310.01  tabletop
    3     310    Polanski  RAL5447   oak pedestal table   310.02  pedestal
    4     310    Alvarez   CH1443    oak pedestal table   310.02  pedestal
    5     310    Polanski  RAL5447   oak pedestal table   310.03  2 leaves
    6     310    Alvarez   CH1443    oak pedestal table   310.03  2 leaves
    7     312    Corrigan  DUR5523   brass floor lamp     312.01  lamp base
    8     312    Corrigan  DUR5523   brass floor lamp     312.02  lamp shade
    9     313    Corrigan  DUR5524   oak bookcase, short  313.01  bookcase
   10     313    Polanski  RAL5498   oak bookcase, short  313.01  bookcase
   11     313    Corrigan  DUR5524   oak bookcase, short  313.02  2 shelves
   12     313    Polanski  RAL5498   oak bookcase, short  313.02  2 shelves
```

Program

The objective is to create a shipping list data set from one data set that shows each item sold and from another data set that shows how many pieces need to be packed for shipping each item. For example, an observation in SALES shows that an oak pedestal table, item 310, was sold, and STOCK shows that item 310 consists of three pieces: a top, a base, and two leaves. The resulting data set SHIPLIST, therefore, will contain three observations for the first sold item recorded in SALES.

First, SALES must be sorted by PRODUCT, and STOCK must be indexed on PRODUCT. In the DATA step, read observations sequentially from SALES, using the SET statement to read one observation on each DATA step iteration. Specify PRODUCT in the BY statement so that you can use BY-group processing.

Then read observations from STOCK directly. Use the SET statement and specify PRODUCT as the key variable with the KEY= option. Place this statement in a DO UNTIL loop that executes until there are no matches in STOCK for the current value of PRODUCT in SALES. Each time a match is found, write an observation to SHIPLIST. When no match occurs, take one of two actions based on whether you've finished processing the current BY group in SALES.

If the current observation is the last observation in SALES for the current BY group, the DO UNTIL loop condition is met and the loop ends and processing returns to the top of the DATA step to read the first observation from the next BY group in SALES.

If the current observation is *not* the last observation in SALES for the current BY group, you must force the pointer to return to the beginning of the index so that observations with matching PRODUCT values in STOCK will be found and matched with observations from SALES. See "A Closer Look" for more detail.

Create SHIPLIST. Read an observation from SALES. Specify PRODUCT as the BY variable. Set DUMMY to 0 at the top of each DATA step iteration. (The next DO loop uses the value of DUMMY.)

```
data shiplist(drop=dummy);
   set sales;
   by product;
   dummy=0;
```

🔲 *Attempt to read an observation from STOCK, based on the value of the key variable PRODUCT. Repeat the process until the value of PRODUCT from SALES does not match any value of PRODUCT from STOCK. When DUMMY is true (equals 1), set PRODUCT to a nonexistent value.* The DO UNTIL loop executes and processes observations from STOCK until no observations contain the current value of PRODUCT. (For information on _IORC_ and %SYSRC, see the Appendix.) DUMMY is true when there are more consecutive observations in SALES that contain the same value for PRODUCT. Set PRODUCT to a nonexistent value. Changing the value of the KEY= variable forces the pointer to return to the beginning of the index, so that later observations in SALES can find matches for the same value of PRODUCT in STOCK.

Use the value of _IORC_ to conditionally process observations. When the value of PRODUCT from SALES matches a PRODUCT value from STOCK, write an observation to SHIPLIST. When the value of _IORC_ corresponds to _SOK, the value of PRODUCT in the observation being read from STOCK matches the current PRODUCT value from SALES.

🔲 *When the current observation from SALES has no matching value for PRODUCT in STOCK, set _ERROR_ to 0. If the current observation from SALES is not the last in the current BY group and if DUMMY is not true (does not equal 1), then set the values of DUMMY and _IORC_ accordingly.* When the value of _IORC_ corresponds to _DSENOM, no observation in STOCK contains the current value of PRODUCT from SALES. _ERROR_ is reset to 0 to prevent an error condition that would write the contents of the program data vector to the SAS log.

In case of an unexpected _IORC_ condition, write an error message and stop execution. When _IORC_ corresponds to anything other than _DSENOM or _SOK, an unexpected condition has occurred, so an error message is written to the SAS log and the STOP statement terminates the DATA step.

```
  do until(_iorc_=%sysrc(_dsenom));
    if dummy then product=99999;
    set stock key=product;



















    select (_iorc_);
       when (%sysrc(_sok)) output;









       when (%sysrc(_dsenom))
          do;
             _error_=0;
             if not last.product and not dummy then
                do;
                   dummy=1;
                   _iorc_=0;
                end;
          end;




       otherwise
          do;
             put 'Unexpected ERROR: _IORC_ =  ' _iorc_;
             stop;
          end;
    end;      /* ends the SELECT group  */
  end;        /* ends the DO UNTIL loop */
run;
```

☒ **A Closer Look**

Finding a Match for Consecutive Duplicate Values

Much of the logic of this program focuses on the need to successfully match observations containing consecutive duplicate values of the BY variable PRODUCT in SALES with observations in STOCK that contain the same value for PRODUCT. Unless you reposition the pointer at the beginning of the PRODUCT index for STOCK, consecutive duplicate values of PRODUCT in SALES will not be successfully matched.

The SELECT group in the DO UNTIL loop begins this process. When there are no more matches in the index on STOCK for the current value of PRODUCT in SALES, determine if there are more observations in the current BY group in SALES. If there are more observations to process in the same BY group in SALES and DUMMY has not already been set to 1, assign values to _IORC_ and the variable DUMMY:

```
when (%sysrc(_dsenom))
    do;
        _error_=0;
        if not last.product and not dummy then
            do;
                dummy=1;
                _iorc_=0;
            end;
    end;
```

By changing the value of _IORC_ to 0, you cause the DO UNTIL loop to iterate again:

```
do until(_iorc_=%sysrc(_dsenom));
    if dummy then product=99999;
    set stock key=product;
```

Because DUMMY is true (equals 1), PRODUCT is set to 99999, a nonexisting value. When the SET statement executes again, the pointer is forced to the beginning of the index on STOCK because the value of PRODUCT (the KEY= variable) has changed. No match is found for 99999, so the DO UNTIL loop ends and processing returns to the top of the DATA step. Then the next observation is read from SALES:

```
data shiplist(drop=dummy);
    set sales;
    by product;
    dummy=0;
```

Because the pointer is at the beginning of the index on STOCK, the observation with a consecutive duplicate value for PRODUCT in SALES finds the appropriate match in STOCK. DUMMY is reset to 0 at the top of the DATA step so that its value does not trigger a change in the value of PRODUCT when it is not needed.

Related Technique

If you are familiar with Structured Query Language (SQL), you may want to use PROC SQL instead of the DATA step. PROC SQL joins the tables[*] to produce a new table, SHIPLST, which includes information from both input tables.

Conceptually, the join results in an internal table that matches every row in SALES with every row in STOCK. However, you want only the rows where the values for PRODUCT are the same in both tables. The WHERE clause returns the rows from the join that have the same values for PRODUCT:

```
proc sql;
   create table shiplst as
      select *
         from sales as a, stock as b
            where a.product=b.product;
quit;
```

Note: In PROC SQL, SELECT *statements* automatically produce a report. SELECT *clauses*, which follow CREATE TABLE or CREATE VIEW statements, do not automatically produce a report.

---

[*] A PROC SQL table is a SAS data set. In SQL terminology, columns are variables and rows are observations.

Example 4.7

Combining Multiple Data Sets without a Variable Common to All the Data Sets

Goal

Combine three tables* that do not share a common column. One table has one column in common with each of the other tables. Use this relationship to combine all three tables. Group the data and use a summary function to summarize numeric data for each group.

Strategy

Join the three tables using the SQL procedure. Use the compound WHERE clause to create a three-way join. Use the GROUP BY clause to group the data. Summarize the numeric data in the groups using the SUM function.

You do not have to sort the data prior to joining the tables.

Input Data Sets

The DAILY table has the ITEMNO column in common with the PRICES table and IDNUM in common with the EMPLOYEE table. In EMPLOYEE, the ID column matches the IDNUM column in DAILY.

EMPLOYEE

OBS	ID	NAME	EMPTYPE	LOCATION
1	341	Kreuger, John	H	Bldg A, Rm 1111
2	511	Olszweski, Joe	S	Bldg A, Rm 1234
3	5112	Nuhn, Len	S	Bldg A, Rm 2123
4	5132	Nguyen, Luan	S	Bldg B, Rm 5022
5	5151	Oveida, Susan	S	Bldg D, Rm 2013
6	3551	Sook, Joy	H	Bldg E, Rm 2533
7	3782	Comuzzi, James	S	Bldg E, Rm 1101
8	381	Smith, Ann	S	Bldg C, Rm 3321

---

*   A PROC SQL table is a SAS data set. In SQL terminology, columns are variables and rows are observations.

DAILY

OBS	IDNUM	ITEMNO	QUANTITY
1	341	101	2
2	341	103	1
3	511	101	1
4	511	103	1
5	5112	105	1
6	5132	105	1
7	3551	104	1
8	3551	105	2
9	3782	104	1
10	341	101	2
11	511	101	1
12	511	103	3
13	5112	105	1
14	5112	101	3
15	5132	105	2
16	3551	104	1
17	3551	105	2
18	3551	103	2
19	3782	104	1
20	3782	105	3

PRICES

OBS	ITEMNO	PRICE
1	101	0.30
2	102	0.65
3	103	2.75
4	104	1.25
5	105	0.85

Resulting Data Set

Output 4.7   CHARGE Table

```
                                    CHARGE
   OBS   ID    NAME             LOCATION        TOTAL    TYPE

    1    341   Kreuger, John    Bldg A, Rm 1111  $3.95   cash charge
    2    3551  Sook, Joy        Bldg E, Rm 2533  $11.40  cash charge
    3    3782  Comuzzi, James   Bldg E, Rm 1101  $5.05   payroll deduction
    4    511   Olszweski, Joe   Bldg A, Rm 1234  $11.60  payroll deduction
    5    5112  Nuhn, Len        Bldg A, Rm 2123  $2.60   payroll deduction
    6    5132  Nguyen, Luan     Bldg B, Rm 5022  $2.55   payroll deduction
```

Program

The objective is to join the EMPLOYEE, DAILY, AND PRICES tables to learn the total charges for each employee. Use the common columns to join all three tables.* As a result of the join, all columns from all three tables are available to process. By joining DAILY and PRICES, you can multiply QUANTITY and PRICE to get a dollar amount for each purchase. By joining DAILY and EMPLOYEE, you can get the name of the employee who made each purchase.

Group the rows so that you can perform a summary calculation on each group and get the total charges for each employee. Grouping the data also eliminates duplicate rows.

Two employees, **381** and **5151**, have no charges in the DAILY table. Therefore, there are no rows with these two IDNUMs that satisfy the WHERE conditions:

Invoke PROC SQL and create a table. The CREATE TABLE statement creates the table CHARGE to store the results of the subsequent query.

```
proc sql;
    create table charge as
```

Begin to specify the columns to be in the query result. Because ID, NAME, and LOCATION occur only in the EMPLOYEE table, you do not have to prefix the table alias to their names.

```
    select id, name, location,
```

Create a new column with an arithmetic expression. The SUM function sums the values that result from multiplying QUANTITY and PRICE. The column TOTAL shows the total charges for each employee. Because the data are grouped, the value of TOTAL is for each group. (If the data were not grouped, the value of TOTAL would be the total for the entire table.)

```
        sum(quantity*price) as total format=dollar8.2,
```

Create a column from EMPTYPE. The CASE expression creates a character column, TYPE, based on the values of EMPTYPE.

```
        case emptype
            when 'H' then 'cash charge'
            when 'S' then 'payroll deduction'
            else 'special'
        end as type
```

Name the tables to join and query. The number of tables that are specified in the FROM clause indicate how many tables you are joining. The AS clause specifies an alias for each table. Table aliases provide a shorthand method for referring to a table in other clauses.

```
    from employee as e, daily as d, prices as p
```

---

* The columns that you join on do not have to have the same name.

Join the tables. ITEMNO is common to the DAILY and PRICES tables. IDNUM and ID are common columns in the DAILY and EMPLOYEE tables, respectively.

```
where p.itemno=d.itemno and id=idnum
```

Group the data to get the total for each employee. The GROUP BY clause returns one row for each employee. In the GROUP BY clause, if you list each column specified in the SELECT clause, PROC SQL has to make only one pass of the data.

```
      group by id, name, location, type;
quit;
```

Note: In PROC SQL, SELECT *statements* automatically produce a report. SELECT *clauses*, which follow CREATE TABLE or CREATE VIEW statements, do not automatically produce a report.

Example 4.8

Interleaving Nonsorted Data Sets

Goal

Combine two tables* that contain columns with the same names. Create a new table from the result. Put the data in order according to the values of two of the columns.

Strategy

PROC SQL provides set operators that enable you to work with the results of two independent queries. Use the OUTER UNION set operator to concatenate the two independent query results returned by the SELECT clauses. Use the CORR keyword to overlay like-named columns.

Input Data Sets

		ONE					TWO		
OBS	DATE	DEPART	FLIGHT		OBS	DATE	DEPART	FLIGHT
1	01JAN93	7:10	114		1	01JAN93	8:21	176
2	01JAN93	10:43	202		2	02JAN93	9:10	176
3	01JAN93	12:16	439		3	03JAN93	8:21	176
4	02JAN93	7:10	114		4	04JAN93	9:31	176
5	02JAN93	10:45	202		5	05JAN93	8:13	176

Resulting Data Set

Output 4.8a　SCHEDULE Data Set
SCHEDULE was created with PROC SQL.

	SCHEDULE		
OBS	DATE	DEPART	FLIGHT
1	01JAN93	7:10	114
2	01JAN93	8:21	176
3	01JAN93	10:43	202
4	01JAN93	12:16	439
5	02JAN93	7:10	114
6	02JAN93	9:10	176
7	02JAN93	10:45	202
8	03JAN93	8:21	176
9	04JAN93	9:31	176
10	05JAN93	8:13	176

---

*　A PROC SQL table is a SAS data set. In SQL terminology, columns are variables and rows are observations.

Output 4.8b SCHED Data Set
SCHED was created with the DATA step.

```
                           SCHED

          OBS     DATE     DEPART    FLIGHT

            1    01JAN93     7:10      114
            2    01JAN93     8:21      176
            3    01JAN93    10:43      202
            4    01JAN93    12:16      439
            5    02JAN93     7:10      114
            6    02JAN93     9:10      176
            7    02JAN93    10:45      202
            8    03JAN93     8:21      176
            9    04JAN93     9:31      176
           10    05JAN93     8:13      176
```

Program

The objective is to combine the tables so that all the flight information is in one table.

To make the table more useful, order the data by the date, and then by the departure time:

Invoke PROC SQL and create a table. The CREATE TABLE statement creates the table SCHEDULE to store the results of the subsequent queries and set operation.

```
proc sql;
   create table schedule as
```

Select all columns from table ONE.

```
      select *
         from one
```

Concatenate the two query results. The OUTER UNION set operator concatenates the queries returned by the two SELECT clauses. CORR overlays columns that have the same name. This operator must come between the two SELECT clauses.

```
      outer union corr
```

Select all columns from table TWO.

```
      select *
         from two
```

Order the concatenation by the values of DATE and DEPART. Without ORDER BY, the rows from table TWO appear after all of the rows from table ONE.

```
      order by date, depart;
quit;
```

Note: In PROC SQL, SELECT *statements* automatically produce a report. SELECT *clauses*, which follow CREATE TABLE or CREATE VIEW statements, do not automatically produce a report.

Related Technique

Using OUTER UNION CORR is equivalent to using the SET statement in the DATA step. The DATA step requires that the data be sorted by the BY variables. This DATA step produces the same output as the PROC SQL step:

```
data sched;
   set one two;
   by date depart;
run;
```

Note: If you use PROC SQL, you do not have to sort or index the data. If the data sets are *not* sorted (regardless of being indexed), it is typically more efficient to use PROC SQL. If the data sets are sorted, it is typically more efficient to use the DATA step and the SET statement.

Example 4.9

Interleaving Data Sets Based on a Common Variable

Goal

Interleave two data sets containing a common variable. Also, demonstate that testing the value of an existing variable instead of a new variable can produce unexpected results when using BY-group processing.

Strategy

Sort the input data by the BY variable. Specify both input data sets in a single SET statement. Use the IN= data set option with one of the data sets to create a variable that indicates when that data set has contributed to an observation.

Two examples of the same program illustrate how unexpected results can occur. The first program tests the value of and updates a variable read from the input data set. It produces unexpected results. The revised version produces accurate results by testing and resetting the value of a variable created during the DATA step.

CAUTION!

Variables read from input SAS data sets are retained across DATA step iterations. Testing or resetting those variables can produce unexpected results. ■

Input Data Sets

Data sets ONE_A, ONE_B, and TWO contain the variable COMMON. Data set ONE_A contains the variable TEST while ONE_B does not. The first program reads data set ONE_A and produces unexpected results. Both programs use data set TWO.

ONE_A

OBS	COMMON	TEST
1	A	AAAA
2	C	CCCC

TWO

OBS	COMMON	SWITCH
1	A	N
2	A	Y
3	A	N
4	B	N
5	B	Y
6	B	N

ONE_B

OBS	COMMON
1	A
2	C

Desired Results

Output 4.9a COMBINED Data Set

TEST contains the value TRUE only in observations 3 and 6.

```
                       COMBINED

          OBS    COMMON    SWITCH    TEST

           1       A
           2       A         N
           3       A         Y        TRUE
           4       A         N
           5       B         N
           6       B         Y        TRUE
           7       B         N
           8       C
```

Original Program

The objective is to interleave data sets ONE_A and TWO, based on the values of the BY variable COMMON. Read the input data sets with BY-group processing by using the SET and BY statements. Use the IN= data set option to create variable IN2, which will be set to 1 (true) for each observation that originates from data set TWO. With an IF statement, test the value of IN2 and the value of the variable SWITCH to determine whether to set the value of the existing variable TEST to 'TRUE':

Create COMBINED. Read an observation from data set ONE_A and data set TWO, using BY group processing. Variable IN2 will be set to 1 for each observation to which TWO contributes. COMMON is the BY variable.

If data set TWO has contributed to an observation (IN2 is true) and if the value of SWITCH is 'Y', then set the current value of TEST to 'TRUE'. The assignment statement assigns a value to the existing variable TEST.

```
data combined;
    set one_a two(in=in2);
    by common;



    if in2 and switch = 'Y' then test = 'TRUE';
run;
```

Unexpected Results

Output 4.9b COMBINED Data Set

In observations 4 and 7, TEST incorrectly contains the value TRUE. Only observations 3 and 6 should contain this value.

```
                       COMBINED

          OBS    COMMON    TEST     SWITCH

           1       A       AAAA
           2       A                 N
           3       A       TRUE      Y
           4       A       TRUE      N
           5       B                 N
           6       B       TRUE      Y
           7       B       TRUE      N
           8       C       CCCC
```

At first glance, Output 4.9b *seems* to show that the IF condition did not work correctly since observations 4 and 7 contain the incorrect value of TRUE. Actually, these observations contain incorrect values for TEST because its value is retained in the program data vector throughout the life of the current BY group. It is replaced only when a new observation is read from data set ONE_A. Because TWO contains multiple observations with the same value of the BY variable while ONE_A contains unique values of the BY variable, the value of TEST is duplicated across all remaining observations in the current BY group.

Revised Program

The revised program uses the same code, but different input data. It reads data set ONE_B, which does not contain TEST. This program tests and changes the value of TEST as a variable that is created *during* the DATA step, *not* read from an existing SAS data set. The assignment statement creates TEST in this example. Its value, therefore, is *not* retained throughout the current BY group, so testing and setting its value does not produce incorrect results when subsequent observations in the same BY group are read from data set TWO. See Output 4.9a.

Create COMBINED. Read an observation from data set ONE_B and data set TWO, using BY-group processing. Variable IN2 will be set to 1 for each observation to which TWO contributes. COMMON is the BY variable.

```
data combined;
   set one_b two(in=in2);
   by common;
```

If data set TWO has contributed to an observation (IN2 is true) and if the value of SWITCH is 'Y', then assign TEST a value of 'TRUE'. The assignment statement creates TEST and assigns it a value. Its value is reset to missing upon each iteration of the DATA step.

```
   if in2 and switch = 'Y' then test = 'TRUE';
run;
```

Example 4.10

Comparing All Observations with the Same BY Values

Goal

Create a new data set by merging two data sets, each of which may contain multiple observations with the same BY values, and by comparing all observations with the same BY values.

Strategy

Begin with two data sets that may contain multiple observations for each unique value of the common variable. In the DATA step, read these data sets to create new data sets that contain one observation per BY group, with variables whose values identify the observation number of the first and last observation for each BY group. Merge these two new data sets so that all the information about BY groups in both data sets is in one location. Include only observations to which the first data set contributed.

To create the final data set, read all three data sets: the two original ones and the merged one that identifies the first and last observation in each BY group. Because each of the original data sets may contain multiple observations with duplicate values of the BY variable, you must loop through the BY groups in each data set multiple times to compare each observation in a given BY group with each observation in the same BY group in the other data set. Therefore, use the POINT= option to directly access *both* data sets by observation number.

You can perform the same task with PROC SQL; see "Related Technique."

Note: Due to the variability of data and the number of conditions that determine the path chosen by the PROC SQL optimizer, it is not always possible to determine the most efficient method without first testing with your data.

Input Data Sets

Both BREAKDWN and MAINT contain multiple observations for certain values of the BY variable VEHICLE. Each is sorted by VEHICLE. Within VEHICLE, each is also sorted by date of breakdown (BRKDNDT) or maintenance (MNTDATE).

	BREAKDWN			MAINT	
OBS	BRKDNDT	VEHICLE	OBS	MNTDATE	VEHICLE
1	02MAR94	AAA	1	03JAN94	AAA
2	20MAY94	AAA	2	05APR94	AAA
3	19JUN94	AAA	3	10AUG94	AAA
4	29NOV94	AAA	4	28JAN94	CCC
5	04JUL94	BBB	5	16MAY94	CCC
6	31MAY94	CCC	6	07OCT94	CCC
7	24DEC94	CCC	7	24FEB94	DDD
			8	22JUN94	DDD
			9	19SEP94	DDD

BRKKEY and MAINTKEY identify the observation number of the first and last observation for each BY group.

	BRKKEY					MAINTKEY		
OBS	VEHICLE	FIRST1	LAST1		OBS	VEHICLE	FIRST2	LAST2
1	AAA	1	4		1	AAA	1	3
2	BBB	5	5		2	CCC	4	6
3	CCC	6	7		3	DDD	7	9

KEYS is the result of merging BRKKEY and MAINTKEY.

	KEYS				
OBS	VEHICLE	FIRST1	LAST1	FIRST2	LAST2
1	AAA	1	4	1	3
2	BBB	5	5	.	.
3	CCC	6	7	4	6

Resulting Data Sets

Output 4.10a FINAL1 Data Set

FINAL1 was created with the DATA step.

```
                        FINAL1
        OBS    VEHICLE    BRKDNDT    LASTMNT
         1       AAA      02MAR94    03JAN94
         2       AAA      20MAY94    05APR94
         3       AAA      19JUN94    05APR94
         4       AAA      29NOV94    10AUG94
         5       BBB      04JUL94       .
         6       CCC      31MAY94    16MAY94
         7       CCC      24DEC94    07OCT94
```

Output 4.10b FINAL2 Data Set

FINAL2 was created with PROC SQL.

```
                        FINAL2
        OBS    VEHICLE    BRKDNDT    LASTMNT
         1       AAA      02MAR94    03JAN94
         2       AAA      20MAY94    05APR94
         3       AAA      19JUN94    05APR94
         4       AAA      29NOV94    10AUG94
         5       BBB      04JUL94       .
         6       CCC      31MAY94    16MAY94
         7       CCC      24DEC94    07OCT94
```

Program

The objective is to create a data set that shows the most recent maintenance date for each time a vehicle had a breakdown.

First, create data sets (BRKKEY and MAINTKEY) that contain one observation for each BY group and two additional variables that identify the observation numbers of the first and last observations for that BY group. Merge these two data sets into a single data set (KEYS) so that you will be able to compare all observations in each BY group between the two data sets. Then read this merged data set and use the FIRST1, LAST1, FIRST2, and LAST2 values to directly access all observations in each BY group in data sets BREAKDWN and MAINT. Then compare the values of MNTDATE and BRKDNDT so that you can determine the correct value for LASTMNT, the most recent maintenance date prior to each time the vehicle needed repairs.

Create BRKKEY. Read an observation from BREAKDWN, using VEHICLE as the BY variable. Create variables FIRST1 and LAST1 whose values represent the observation number of the first and last observation in each BY group. After reading the last observation in each BY group, write an observation that includes only VEHICLE and FIRST1 and LAST1. RETAIN retains the value of FIRST1 across DATA step iterations so that it is still available when LAST1 obtains a value and the observation is written.

```
data brkkey (keep = vehicle first1 last1);
   set breakdwn;
   by vehicle;
   retain first1;
   if first.vehicle then first1=_n_;
   if last.vehicle then
      do;
         last1=_n_;
         output;
      end;
run;
```

Create MAINTKEY. Use the same logic as in the preceding DATA step. In this DATA step, the variables whose values represent the observation number of the first and last observation in each BY group are named FIRST2 and LAST2.

```
data maintkey (keep = vehicle first2 last2);
   set maint;
   by vehicle;
   retain first2;
   if first.vehicle then first2=_n_;
   if last.vehicle then
      do;
         last2=_n_;
         output;
      end;
run;
```

Create KEYS by merging data sets BRKKEY and MAINTKEY, based on the value of VEHICLE. Include only observations to which data set BRKKEY contributed. The IN= data set option creates a variable that is set to a value of 1 for each iteration in which data set BRKKEY contributes to the current observation. The subsetting IF statement allows only observations to which BRKKEY contributed to be written to KEYS.

```
data keys;
   merge brkkey(in=in1) maintkey;
   by vehicle;
   if in1;
run;
```

Create FINAL1. Read an observation from KEYS. Each iteration of this DATA step processes an entire BY group.

Read an observation from BREAKDWN in the current BY group. POINT= enables you to read data set BREAKDWN using direct access. For each DATA step iteration, this DO loop reads all observations in the current BY group in BREAKDWN. LASTMNT is initialized to missing for each observation in the current BY group of BREAKDWN in preparation for determining the most recent MNTDATE in MAINT prior to the current BRKDNDT from BREAKDWN.

```
data final1;
   drop first1 last1 first2 last2 mntdate;
   set keys;

   do i=first1 to last1;
      set breakdwn point=i;
      format lastmnt date7.;
      lastmnt=. ;
```

If data set MAINT contributed to the current observation, then execute this nested DO loop to process all observations from MAINT for this BY group. On each iteration, read an observation from MAINT and compare the values of MNTDATE, LASTMNT, and BRKDNDT. If the MNTDATE value is greater than LASTMNT yet less than BRKDNDT, then set LASTMNT equal to the value of MNTDATE. If MNTDATE is greater than BRKDNDT, then you know there are no more maintenance dates prior to the breakdown date, so stop processing this DO loop. On each DATA step iteration, this DO loop executes if MAINT FIRST2 does not have a missing value. The DO loop reads and processes all observations in the BY group until it reaches a MNTDATE that is past the BRKDNDT or until all observations have been processed. The LEAVE statement allows processing to exit the DO loop and to begin executing the next statement in the DATA step, which writes the current observation to FINAL. Because BREAKDWN is sorted by date of breakdown within VEHICLE, it is appropriate to exit the DO loop when the value of MNTDATE exceeds BRKDNDT.

```
      if first2 ne . then
         do j=first2 to last2;
            set maint point=j;
            if mntdate gt lastmnt and mntdate le brkdndt
               then lastmnt=mntdate;
               else if mntdate gt brkdndt then leave;
         end;
      output;
   end;          /* ends the outer iterative DO loop */
run;
```

Related Technique

If you are familiar with Structured Query Language (SQL), you may want to use PROC SQL instead of the DATA step. PROC SQL joins the tables* to produce a new table, FINAL2. Conceptually, a join results in an internal table that matches every row in BREAKDWN with every row in MAINT.

This example shows a *left join*, which returns all rows that meet the ON clause criteria *and* the rows from the left table (BREAKDWN) that do not match any row in the right table (MAINT).

The ON clause specifies that the resulting table will contain only those rows where the values of VEHICLE match and where the breakdown date is later than the maintenance date.

The HAVING clause ensures that you get the row with the latest maintenance date for each vehicle.

To understand how this join works, consider the matches for the breakdown date of **20MAY94** in the BREAKDWN table. ON specifies that the join will return only rows from the internal table where the value of vehicle is the same

---

* A PROC SQL table is a SAS data set. In SQL terminology, columns are variables and rows are observations.

and where the breakdown date is later than the maintenance date. Only two rows from the internal table meet both of those criteria:

```
VEHICLE    BRKDNDT    LASTMNT

AAA        20MAY94    05APR94
AAA        20MAY94    03JAN94
```

Because the HAVING clause further restricts the result to include only the row that has the *latest* maintenance date, only the shaded row appears in the final result.

The row for vehicle BBB is the only row returned by the join from the left table that does not have a match in the right table.

Here is the PROC SQL step that creates FINAL2:

```
proc sql;
   create table final2 as
      select b.vehicle, b.brkdndt, m.mntdate as lastmnt
         from breakdwn b left join maint m
               on b.vehicle=m.vehicle and b.brkdndt >= m.mntdate
         group by b.vehicle, b.brkdndt
         having m.mntdate = max(m.mntdate);
quit;
```

Note: In PROC SQL, SELECT *statements* automatically produce a report. SELECT *clauses*, which follow CREATE TABLE or CREATE VIEW statements, do not automatically produce a report.

Where to Go from Here

□ **LEAVE statement.** For a complete description with an example, see pp. 34–35 in *SAS Technical Report P-222, Changes and Enhancements to Base SAS Software, Release 6.07.*

C H A P T E R   5

Manipulating Data From a Single Source

You can work with the data in a single data set in many ways to enhance it or reshape it as you need. For example, you can calculate new values from existing variables, apply common operations to a group of variables, collapse observations, or expand observations. For a complete list of the tasks covered in this chapter, see the example titles below:

Example 5.1

Performing a Simple Subset

Goal

Create a subset of a SAS data set efficiently by selecting for processing only observations that meet a particular condition.

Strategy

To subset a SAS data set based on a variable value, you can use the WHERE statement with the SET statement to specify a condition that the data must satisfy before observations are read into the program data vector. Using a WHERE statement is efficient because it takes effect before the SET statement executes on each DATA step iteration. Instead of reading all observations, the SET statement then reads only the observations from the input data set whose data meet the specified condition.

Input Data Sets

NEWHIRES

OBS	NAME	DEPT	ID
1	Estefon, Emilio	Toys	54345
2	Wentworth, Guy	Hardware	43454
3	Nay, Rong	Automotive	23234
4	Harper, Chang	Toys	45434
5	Smart, Matthew	Toys	45412
6	Ochman, Andre	Toys	45413
7	Welk, Liz Ann	Hardware	32322
8	Jordan, Erica	Linens	31012

Resulting Data Set

Output 5.1   TOYDEPT Data Set

TOYDEPT

OBS	NAME	DEPT	ID
1	Estefon, Emilio	Toys	54345
2	Harper, Chang	Toys	45434
3	Smart, Matthew	Toys	45412
4	Ochman, Andre	Toys	45413

Program

Create TOYDEPT. Read an observation from NEWHIRES only if the employee works in the toy department. The WHERE statement prevents unneeded observations from being read into the program data vector.

The objective is to create a subset of the data set NEWHIRES that includes only employees in the Toys department. The WHERE statement allows only observations that have a value of **Toys** for DEPT to be read by the SET statement:

```
data toydept;
   set newhires;
   where dept='Toys';
run;
```

Example 5.2

Separating Unique Observations from Duplicate Observations

Goal

Identify duplicate and nonduplicate observations in a data set and write each to the appropriate data set.

Strategy

Sort the input data set by the BY variables. Read the input data set with the SET and BY statements. Use the FIRST. and LAST. variables for the appropriate BY variable to determine when an entire observation is a duplicate in the data set. When both FIRST.*variable* and LAST.*variable* for the appropriate BY variable are equal to 1 (true), then you know that the observation is not a duplicate so write it to a data set. Write all other observations to a data set for duplicates.

Input Data Sets

CLASDATA must be sorted by NAME and CLASS within NAME.

CLASDATA

OBS	ID	NAME	CLASS
1	3456	Amber	CHEM101
2	3456	Amber	MATH102
3	3456	Amber	MATH102
4	4567	Denise	ENGL201
5	4567	Denise	ENGL201
6	2345	Ginny	CHEM101
7	2345	Ginny	ENGL201
8	2345	Ginny	MATH102
9	1234	Lynn	CHEM101
10	1234	Lynn	CHEM101
11	1234	Lynn	MATH102
12	5678	Rick	CHEM101
13	5678	Rick	HIST300
14	5678	Rick	HIST300

Resulting Data Sets

Output 5.2a   DUPS Data Set

DUPS

OBS	ID	NAME	CLASS
1	3456	Amber	MATH102
2	3456	Amber	MATH102
3	4567	Denise	ENGL201
4	4567	Denise	ENGL201
5	1234	Lynn	CHEM101
6	1234	Lynn	CHEM101
7	5678	Rick	HIST300
8	5678	Rick	HIST300

Output 5.2b NODUPS Data Set

```
                          NODUPS

           OBS    ID     NAME     CLASS

            1    3456   Amber    CHEM101
            2    2345   Ginny    CHEM101
            3    2345   Ginny    ENGL201
            4    2345   Ginny    MATH102
            5    1234   Lynn     MATH102
            6    5678   Rick     CHEM101
```

Program

The objective is to determine which observations in CLASDATA are duplicates. A student's name may be in the data set more than once, but no two observations should contain both the same student name and the class.

First, sort CLASDATA by NAME and CLASS. Then use BY-group processing to create the FIRST. and LAST. variables for the BY variables. When FIRST.CLASS and LAST.CLASS are both equal to 1, you know that the observation is the only one with these values for NAME and CLASS in the data set. Write it to the NODUPS data set. If these variables are not both equal to 1, the observation is a duplicate, so write it to the DUPS data set:

Create DUPS and NODUPS. Read an observation from CLASDATA using the SET statement and BY-group processing. Specify NAME and CLASS as BY variables.

```
data dups nodups;
   set clasdata;
   by name class;
```

Compare the values of the FIRST.CLASS and LAST.CLASS variables. Write an observation to NODUPS or DUPS, depending on the outcome of the comparison.

```
   if first.class and last.class then output nodups;
   else output dups;
run;
```

Example 5.3

Accessing a Specific Number of Observations from the Beginning and End of a Data Set

Goal

Process only the first five and last five observations in a data set efficiently by not reading the entire data set.

Strategy

Process specific observations rather than all observations sequentially by using the POINT= option in the SET statement. Use the NOBS= option in the SET statement to assign to a variable the number of observations in the data set. Use DO loops to read only the first five and last five observations in the data set. Because the application calls for reading at least ten observations, use IF-THEN logic to avoid reading some observations twice when a data set contains fewer than ten observations. Reduce redundancy in your program by using the LINK statement to repeatedly route execution to a group of data-reading and data-writing statements.

Input Data Set

SALES

OBS	NAME	DAYSALES
1	Ball, George	674
2	Lee, Chin	1800
3	Placa, Ace	2500
4	Leung, Ho	3000
5	Wagner, Willie	850
6	DuBois, Grace	2000
7	Jernigan, Alec	750
8	Tilldale, Jules	1000
9	Brown, Dick	555
10	Hammer, Danny	400
11	Wills, Wesley	800
12	Grant, Heber	3500
13	Mooney, Hal	400

Resulting Data Set

Output 5.3 SUBSET Data Set

The first five and last five observations from SALES.

SUBSET

OBS	NAME	DAYSALES
1	Ball, George	674
2	Lee, Chin	1800
3	Placa, Ace	2500
4	Leung, Ho	3000
5	Wagner, Willie	850
6	Brown, Dick	555
7	Hammer, Danny	400
8	Wills, Wesley	800
9	Grant, Heber	3500
10	Mooney, Hal	400

Program

The objective is to create a subset of the SALES data set that contains only the first five and last five observations. Because SALES has more than ten observations, you must set the values of the variables STARTOBS and ENDOBS to indicate which observations to read: the first five observations and the last five observations. After these values are set, link to a set of labelled statements that read and write five observations.

If SALES has fewer than ten observations, you can simply read from the beginning to the end of the data set. However, by using the same method of access, direct instead of sequential, regardless of the size of the data set, you can link to the same block of data-reading and data-writing statements, making your code more compact:

Create SUBSET.

```
data subset (drop=startobs endobs);
```

For data sets with more than ten observations, process the first five and last five observations. The assignment statements set the appropriate values for STARTOBS and ENDOBS, which will be used to control the DO loop that reads and writes observations. The first LINK statement causes the statements that follow the label GETOBS to execute and process the first five observations. Execution then returns to the statement following the LINK statement. The STARTOBS and ENDOBS values are reset, based on the value of NUMOBS, the NOBS= variable. (See the SET statement later in this program.) When the program is compiled, NUMOBS is assigned a value equal to the number of observations in data set SALES. The second LINK statement causes the labeled statements to execute again, this time processing the last five observations.

```
   if numobs > 10 then
      do;
         startobs=1;
         endobs=5;
         link getobs;
         startobs=numobs-4;
         endobs=numobs;
         link getobs;
      end;
```

For data sets with ten or fewer observations, process all observations. The LINK statement causes the statements that follow the label GETOBS to execute and process all of the observations in data set SALES.

```
   else
      do;
         startobs=1;
         endobs=numobs;
         link getobs;
      end;
```

Prevent the DATA step from continuous looping. Because there is no end-of-file condition when direct access is used to read data, you must use a STOP statement to prevent continuous looping. (See the SET statement with the POINT= option later in the program.)

```
   stop;
```

***Read and write each observation, as
indicated by the values of STARTOBS and
ENDOBS.*** The LINK GETOBS statements
cause these statements to execute. The
POINT= option makes direct access
possible. The NOBS option creates a
variable named NUMOBS whose value is
the number of observations in the SALES
data set. The RETURN statement that
precedes the label prevents any statements
that follow the label from executing, except
when a LINK statement routes execution
there. (This RETURN statement is not
necessary in this program, but using it is
good practice because it's often necessary.)
The final RETURN statement signals the
end of the section labeled GETOBS and
routes execution to the statement following
the LINK statement that linked to this block
of code.

```
return;
getobs:
   do i=startobs to endobs;
      set sales point=i nobs=numobs;
      output;
   end;
return;
run;
```

Example 5.4

Adding New Observations to the End of a Data Set

Goal

Add new observations to the end of a data set, while retaining the original name of the data set.

Strategy

Use the END= option in the SET statement to determine when the end of the data set has been reached. Then use a DO loop to generate new observations and append them to the end of the data set. If you want the resulting data set to retain the same name, specify the same data set name in the DATA and SET statements.

You can also create a new data set to contain the new observations and then add those to the original data set by using PROC APPEND. See "Related Technique."

Input Data Set

```
      TEST1

OBS    X    Y

 1     1    2
 2     2    4
 3     3    6
 4     4    8
 5     5   10
```

Resulting Data Set

Output 5.4a   TEST1 Data Set, New Version

TEST1 was produced with the DATA step.

```
              TEST1

        OBS    X    Y

         1     1    2
         2     2    4
         3     3    6
         4     4    8
         5     5   10
         6     6   12
         7     7   14
         8     8   16
         9     9   18
        10    10   20
        11    11   22
        12    12   24
        13    13   26
        14    14   28
        15    15   30
```

Output 5.4b   TEST1 Data Set, New
Version

TEST1 was produced with the DATA step
and PROC APPEND.

```
                          TEST1

                  OBS     X     Y

                   1      1     2
                   2      2     4
                   3      3     6
                   4      4     8
                   5      5    10
                   6      6    12
                   7      7    14
                   8      8    16
                   9      9    18
                  10     10    20
                  11     11    22
                  12     12    24
                  13     13    26
                  14     14    28
                  15     15    30
```

Program

The objective is to use the value of the END= variable to determine when the
last observation from TEST1 has been read. Then execute an iterative DO loop
to generate ten new observations and add them to the end of TEST1.

You can also use a DATA step to create the new data set and PROC APPEND
to add observations from the second data set to the end of the first one. See
"Related Technique."

***Specify an output data set with the same
name as the input data set. Read an
observation from TEST1.*** END= defines a
variable (LASTONE) that is set to 1 when
the last observation has been read from
TEST1. The OUTPUT statement is required
because use of an explicit OUTPUT
statement in the DO loop disables the
automatic OUTPUT executed for each
iteration of the DATA step.

```
data test1(drop=i);
   set test1 end=lastone;
   output;
```

***After the last observation has been read,
generate new observations and write them
to TEST1.*** When LASTONE equals 1, this
DO loop executes to assign values to X and
Y and to write ten new observations.

```
   if lastone then do;
      do i=1 to 10;
         x=x+1;
         y=y+2;
         output;
      end;
   end;
run;
```

Related Technique

If your original data set is very large, it is probably more efficient to use a DATA step to create the additional observations and then add them to the end of the original data set by using PROC APPEND. So that you can initialize the values of X and Y to their values in the last observation of TEST1, read only that observation from TEST1 on the first iteration. Use a DO loop to create ten new observations. Because there is no end-of-file condition to stop this DATA step, you must use a STOP statement:

```
data test2(drop=i);
    if _n_=1 then set test1 point=lastobs nobs=lastobs;
    do i = 1 to 10;
        x = x +1;
        y = y + 2;
        output;
    end;
    stop;
run;

proc append base=test1 data=test2;
run;
```

Example 5.5

Adding Observations to a Data Set Based on the Value of a Variable

Goal

Add a specific number of observations to a data set, based on the value of one of its variables, so that the resulting data set retains the name of the original.

Strategy

Read an observation from the data set. Use the value of an existing variable to determine how many times the DO loop should iterate and write an observation. If you want the resulting data set to have the same name, specify the same data set name in the DATA and SET statements.

Input Data Set

Each observation has a unique value for JOB.

TASKS

OBS	DAYS	JOB
1	1	wiring
2	2	drywall
3	4	flooring
4	2	trimwork
5	3	painting

Resulting Data Set

Output 5.5   TASKS Data Set, New Version

TASKS

OBS	DATE	DAYS	JOB
1	10JUL1995	1	wiring
2	11JUL1995	2	drywall
3	12JUL1995	2	drywall
4	13JUL1995	4	flooring
5	14JUL1995	4	flooring
6	17JUL1995	4	flooring
7	18JUL1995	4	flooring
8	19JUL1995	2	trimwork
9	20JUL1995	2	trimwork
10	21JUL1995	3	painting
11	24JUL1995	3	painting
12	25JUL1995	3	painting

Program

The objective is to use the value of DAYS to determine how many observations to generate for each JOB and, beginning with the current day, determine on what days the job will be done. The value of DAYS determines how many times the DO loop iterates, writing an observation each time:

Create an output data set with the same name as the original one. Read an observation from TASKS.

```
data tasks(drop=i testday);
   format date date9.;
   set tasks;
```

On the first iteration, set the value of DATE. The TODAY function returns the SAS date value for the current day.

```
   if _n_=1 then date=today();
```

Write one observation for each day that the task requires and increase the DATE value appropriately. Use the WEEKDAY function to derive the day of the week from the DATE variable. If the weekday is Saturday (7) or Sunday (1), then add either 1 or 2 to its value so that the new value is the date for the following Monday (2). The sum statement (**date+1;**) increases the value of DATE by 1 and also causes the value of DATE to be automatically retained across iterations of the DATA step.

```
   do i=1 to days;
      testday=weekday(date);
      if testday=7 then date=date+2;
      if testday=1 then date=date+1;
      output;
      date+1;
   end;
run;
```

Example 5.6

Simulating the LEAD Function by Comparing the Value of a Variable to Its Value in the Next Observation

Goal

Within the same data set, look ahead from a variable value in one observation to return the value of the same variable in the observation that immediately follows it. Then compare the returned value with the current observation or use it in a calculation on the current observation.

Strategy

You can use DATA step processing to simulate the LEAD function. To look ahead from one observation to the next within the same data set, merge the data set with itself by specifying the same data set name twice in the MERGE statement. In the second reference to the data set, use the data set option FIRSTOBS= to start processing with the second observation in the same data set. Because the program does not contain the BY statement, SAS software performs a one-to-one merge, but the pointer in the second reference to the data set will always be one observation ahead of the first reference.

In the second reference to the data set, use the RENAME= and KEEP= options. RENAME= gives the look-ahead variable a unique name, thus preventing the look-ahead value from overwriting the value read from the first reference. KEEP= allows only the look-ahead variable from the second reference to the data set to be brought into the program data vector. If you keep all variables from the look-ahead read, you would overlay values of variables with the same names that you just read from the first reference to the data set.

Input Data Set

ONE

OBS	X	Y
1	5	1
2	5	2
3	10	1
4	2	1
5	2	2
6	19	1

Resulting Data Set

Output 5.6 TWO Data Set

```
                          TWO

          OBS     X    Y    NEXTX    MATCH

           1      5    1      5      YES
           2      5    2     10      NO
           3     10    1      2      NO
           4      2    1      2      YES
           5      2    2     19      NO
           6     19    1      .      NO
```

Program

The objective is to create a new data set, TWO, in which each observation contains the value of X for the current observation and for the next observation. To create data set TWO, merge data set ONE with itself. In the second reference to data set ONE, do three things:

1. Begin reading at the second observation.

2. Rename X to NEXTX so that you can store the look-ahead values of X without overwriting the value of X from the current observation in the first reference.

3. Bring only the look-ahead variable into the program data vector. Otherwise, you would overwrite all the other variables with values from the next observation.

Then use IF-THEN/ELSE logic to compare the original and look-ahead values and to report a match:

Create TWO by merging ONE with itself. Begin reading the second reference to data set ONE with the second observation. Use FIRSTOBS=2 to start the look-ahead process at the second observation. This example looks ahead only one observation, but by setting the FIRSTOBS= option differently, you could read ahead any number of observations. RENAME= renames X so that the look-ahead value doesn't overwrite the current value of X in the program data vector. KEEP= ensures that only the value of X from the look-ahead observation will be brought into the program data vector.

```
data two;
   merge one one(firstobs=2 rename=(x=nextx) keep=x);
```

For each observation, compare the original and look-ahead values of X and create the new variable MATCH to report the comparison.

```
   if x=nextx then match='YES';
   else match='NO';
run;
```

Example 5.7

Obtaining the Lag (Previous Value) of a Variable within a BY Group

Goal

Create lagged values* for variables within a BY group.

Strategy

Use the LAG*n* function in conjunction with BY-group processing and array processing to create lagged values for a variable within each BY group. After each BY group is processed, use an IF-THEN statement to reinitialize the lagged values to missing.

Input Data Set

INFORMS is sorted by START.

INFORMS

OBS	START	END
1	1	2
2	1	1
3	1	3
4	1	4
5	1	10
6	1	5
7	2	1
8	2	2
9	3	1
10	3	3
11	3	2
12	3	4
13	3	5

Resulting Data Set

Output 5.7   SHOWLAG Data Set

SHOWLAG contains lagged values within BY groups, based on START.

SHOWLAG

OBS	START	END	ENDLAG1	ENDLAG2	ENDLAG3	ENDLAG4
1	1	2	.	.	.	.
2	1	1	2	.	.	.
3	1	3	1	2	.	.
4	1	4	3	1	2	.
5	1	10	4	3	1	2
6	1	5	10	4	3	1
7	2	1	.	.	.	.
8	2	2	1	.	.	.
9	3	1	.	.	.	.
10	3	3	1	.	.	.
11	3	2	3	1	.	.
12	3	4	2	3	1	.
13	3	5	4	2	3	1

---

*   A *lagged value* is an earlier value for a given variable.

Program

The objective is to process data set INFORMS in BY groups based on the value of START and create lagged values for END within each BY group. The input data set INFORMS must be sorted by START. Use the LAG*n* function to create the necessary lagged values. Use an array and an iterative DO loop to reset variables that hold lagged values so that lagged values are not held across BY groups.

This program generates up to four lagged values. By increasing the size of the array and the number of assignment statements that use the LAG*n* functions, you can generate as many lagged values as needed:

Create SHOWLAG. Read an observation from INFORMS. Specify START as the BY variable.

```
data showlag(drop=i count);
   set informs;
   by start;
```

Define the array GROUP. Create and assign values to four new variables. Use ENDLAG1–ENDLAG4 to store lagged values of END, from the most recent to the fourth preceding value.

```
   array group (*) endlag1-endlag4;
   endlag1=lag1(end);
   endlag2=lag2(end);
   endlag3=lag3(end);
   endlag4=lag4(end);
```

When the first observation in each BY group is processed, reset COUNT to 1. This value is used by the following DO loop to set appropriate array elements to missing.

```
   if first.start then count=1;
```

On each iteration, set to missing array elements that have not yet received a lagged value for the current BY group. Increase COUNT by 1. If these array elements are not set to missing before an observation is written, they would still contain lagged values from the previous BY group. The DIM function returns the number of elements in an array. Using DIM prevents you from having to change the upper bound of an iterative DO group if you later change the number of array elements.

```
   do i=count to dim(group);
      group(i)=.;
   end;
   count + 1;
run;
```

Example 5.8

Applying Common Operations to a Group of Variables

Goal

Apply an arithmetic operation to selected numeric variables in a data set by using an array without explicitly listing the variable names.

Strategy

Move the variables you do not want processed to the beginning of the program data vector by listing them in the RETAIN statement that precedes the SET statement. Then define a numeric array so that no intervening character variables are processed. By specifying _NUMERIC_, you can define an array of numeric variables without specifying the names of the variables. Set the DO loop to begin with the first variable you want processed.

Input Data Set

GRADES

OBS	NAME	TEST1	TEST2	TEST3	TEST4	TEST5	TEST6	TEST7	TEST8	TEST9	TEST10
1	Betty	78	88	94	57	89	77	79	81	89	82
2	James	74	82	88	71	88	81	72	84	91	77
3	Fred	69	71	81	64	79	74	66	77	81	95

Resulting Data Set

Output 5.8 CURVE Data Set

CURVE contains scores with curved values for seven tests. Scores for Tests 3, 5, and 9 are not curved.

				CURVE							
OBS	TEST3	TEST5	TEST9	NAME	TEST1	TEST2	TEST4	TEST6	TEST7	TEST8	TEST10
1	94	89	89	Betty	88	98	67	87	89	91	92
2	88	88	91	James	84	92	81	91	82	94	87
3	81	79	81	Fred	79	81	74	84	76	87	100

Program

The objective is to curve the values of seven out of ten test scores in a data set. First, move the three scores you don't want curved to the front of the progam data vector by using the RETAIN statement before the SET statement. Then define the array ALLTEST by using _NUMERIC_ so that you do not have to list the numeric variables explicitly. Use a DO loop to begin processing with the fourth numeric element in the ALLTEST array. Then execute whatever formula you want on the fourth through tenth array elements:

Create CURVE. Move variables you don't want processed to the front of the program data vector.

Read an observation from GRADES and define the numeric array ALLTEST.

Process variables in the array ALLTEST, beginning with the fourth element. Apply the curve by adding 10 to each test score. Set all scores above 100 to 100. The DO loop begins with 4 so that the first three numeric variables in the array will not be processed. The DIM function returns the number of elements in an array. Using DIM prevents you from having to change the upper bound of an iterative DO group if you later change the number of array elements.

```
data curve(drop=i);
   retain test3 test5 test9;

   set grades;
   array alltest _numeric_;

   do i=4 to dim(alltest);
      alltest(i)+10;
      if alltest(i) > 100 then alltest(i) = 100;
   end;
run;
```

Example 5.9

Calculating Totals across a BY Group to Produce Either a Grand or Cumulative Total

Goal

Create a data set that collapses each BY group into a single observation and produces grand totals for variables in each BY group. You can also create a new data set that contains cumulative totals for observations within a BY group.

Strategy

The input data must be sorted on the BY variable. In a DATA step, use a BY statement to create FIRST. and LAST. variables for the BY variable. Using the values of these variables with IF-THEN logic, you can process observations in groups. By using SUM statements and creating new variables to contain running totals, you can accumulate the values of each variable as you process the BY groups.

So that the new data set contains only the grand totals for each BY group, use an OUTPUT statement with IF-THEN logic to write only the last observation for each BY group. Rename the original variables if you want the new variables containing the totals to have the same name as the original variables.

To create an output data set that contains only a running or cumulative total for each BY group, remove the IF-THEN logic that causes only the last observation from each BY group to be written to the output data set. See "Related Technique."

Input Data Set

SCORES is sorted by ID.

SCORES

OBS	ID	GAME1	GAME2	GAME3
1	A	2	3	4
2	A	5	6	7
3	B	1	2	3
4	C	1	2	3
5	C	4	5	6
6	C	7	8	9

Resulting Data Set

Output 5.9a GRANDTOT Data Set

GRANDTOT contains the game grand totals for each ID.

GRANDTOT

OBS	ID	GAME1	GAME2	GAME3
1	A	7	9	11
2	B	1	2	3
3	C	12	15	18

Output 5.9b CUMTOT Data Set

Cumulative game totals for each ID.

```
                            CUMTOT

          OBS    ID    GAME1    GAME2    GAME3

           1     A       2        3        4
           2     A       7        9       11
           3     B       1        2        3
           4     C       1        2        3
           5     C       5        7        9
           6     C      12       15       18
```

Program

The objective is to create an output data set that contains the grand totals for the variables GAME1, GAME2, and GAME3 for each BY group. The data must be sorted by ID, the BY variable. Create new variables that will contain accumulated totals. Use IF-THEN processing and the value of FIRST.ID to reset these variables to 0 each time a new BY group begins. Use the SUM statement to create running totals. Use the IF-THEN and OUTPUT statement to write only the last observation for each BY group to the output data set. Rename the original variables from SCORES so that the variables in the new data set that contain the accumulated totals can preserve the original variable names:

Create GRANDTOT and drop the variables that represent the GAME1– GAME3 values from SCORES. Read an observation from SCORES and rename the original variables containing the game score values. The BY statement specifies ID as the BY-group variable and creates the variables FIRST.ID and LAST.ID.

```
data grandtot(drop=temp1 temp2 temp3);
   set scores(rename= (game1=temp1 game2=temp2 game3=temp3));
   by id;
```

When reading the first observation of each BY group, reset the values of GAME1– GAME3 to zero so that the total from the previous BY group is not retained.

```
   if first.id then
      do;
         game1=0;
         game2=0;
         game3=0;
      end;
```

Add the current value of TEMP1–TEMP3 to the running totals. Write only the last observation for each value of ID to GRANDTOT. The three sum statements add the values of TEMP1–TEMP3 to GAME1– GAME3 and also cause the values of GAME1–GAME3 to be automatically retained across iterations of the DATA step.

```
   game1 + temp1;
   game2 + temp2;
   game3 + temp3;
   if last.id then output;
run;
```

Related Technique

You can produce a data set that contains running totals of GAME1–GAME3 for each BY group by removing the last IF-THEN statement from the end of the DATA step in the previous program:

```
if last.id then output;
```

The DATA statement was also changed to produce the CUMTOT data set. See Output 5.9b.

Example 5.10

Calculating the Percentage That One Observation Contributes to the Total of a BY Group

Goal

Calculate BY-group totals for a variable and then create a variable that shows the percentage that each observation contributes to the total for that BY group.

Strategy

Use PROC MEANS to calculate a total for each BY group and to create a new data set that contains one observation for each BY group. Then use a one-to-many merge to merge this data set with the original data set and calculate the percentage that a variable in each observation contributes to the BY-group total. You can calculate this percentage for each observation because match-merging causes the variables to be retained throughout each BY group.

You can perform the same task with PROC SQL. See "Related Technique."

Note: Due to the variability of data and the number of conditions that determine the path chosen by the PROC SQL optimizer, it is not always possible to determine the most efficient method without first testing with your data.

Input Data Sets

Both SALES and REGTOT are sorted by the variable REGION. The REGTOT data set, created with PROC MEANS, contains the total amount of sales for each region.

SALES

OBS	REGION	REPID	AMOUNT
1	EAST	1051	$2,508,000
2	EAST	1055	$1,805,000
3	NORTH	1001	$1,000,000
4	NORTH	1002	$1,100,000
5	NORTH	1003	$1,550,000
6	NORTH	1008	$1,250,000
7	NORTH	1005	$900,000
8	SOUTH	1007	$2,105,000
9	SOUTH	1010	$875,000
10	SOUTH	1012	$1,655,000

REGTOT

OBS	REGION	REGTOTAL
1	EAST	$4,313,000
2	NORTH	$5,800,000
3	SOUTH	$4,635,000

Resulting Data Sets

Output 5.10a PERCENT1 Data Set

PERCENT1 was created with the DATA step.

```
                              PERCENT1

     OBS   REGION   REPID    AMOUNT      REGTOTAL    REGPCT

      1    EAST     1051    $2,508,000   $4,313,000   58.15
      2    EAST     1055    $1,805,000   $4,313,000   41.85
      3    NORTH    1001    $1,000,000   $5,800,000   17.24
      4    NORTH    1002    $1,100,000   $5,800,000   18.97
      5    NORTH    1003    $1,550,000   $5,800,000   26.72
      6    NORTH    1008    $1,250,000   $5,800,000   21.55
      7    NORTH    1005      $900,000   $5,800,000   15.52
      8    SOUTH    1007    $2,105,000   $4,635,000   45.42
      9    SOUTH    1010      $875,000   $4,635,000   18.88
     10    SOUTH    1012    $1,655,000   $4,635,000   35.71
```

Output 5.10b PERCENT2 Data Set

PERCENT2 was created with PROC SQL.

```
                              PERCENT2

     OBS   REGION   REPID    AMOUNT      REGTOTAL    REGPCT

      1    EAST     1051    $2,508,000   $4,313,000   58.15
      2    EAST     1055    $1,805,000   $4,313,000   41.85
      3    NORTH    1001    $1,000,000   $5,800,000   17.24
      4    NORTH    1002    $1,100,000   $5,800,000   18.97
      5    NORTH    1003    $1,550,000   $5,800,000   26.72
      6    NORTH    1008    $1,250,000   $5,800,000   21.55
      7    NORTH    1005      $900,000   $5,800,000   15.52
      8    SOUTH    1007    $2,105,000   $4,635,000   45.42
      9    SOUTH    1010      $875,000   $4,635,000   18.88
     10    SOUTH    1012    $1,655,000   $4,635,000   35.71
```

Program

The objective is to produce a data set that shows not only the sales amount produced by each sales representative but also what percentage it represented in the total for the region.

First, use PROC MEANS to produce REGTOT, an output data set that contains totals calculated for the AMOUNT variable for each BY group in SALES. Then merge REGTOT with SALES by REGION and calculate the percentage of region total (REGTOTAL) for the amount sold by each sales representative.

Due to match-merging behavior, the value of REGTOTAL is retained until the value of the BY variable REGION changes. The value of REGTOTAL, therefore, is available for calculating the value of REGPCT for each observation.

Create REGTOT, a data set that contains one observation for each REGION. Create a new variable, REGTOTAL, that contains the total AMOUNT for each REGION.

```
proc means data=sales noprint nway;
   var amount;
   by region;
   output out=regtot(keep=regtotal region) sum=regtotal;
run;
```

Create PERCENT1 by merging REGTOT with SALES, based on the value of the BY variable REGION.

```
data percent1;
   merge sales regtot;
   by region;

   regpct = (amount / regtotal ) * 100;
   format regpct 6.2 amount regtotal dollar10.;
run;
```

Calculate the percentage each observation contributed to the total for the appropriate region. AMOUNT is the amount contributed by each sales representative and REGTOTAL is the sales total for that region.

Related Technique

If you are familiar with Structured Query Language (SQL), you may want to use PROC SQL instead of the DATA step. Using the SALES table,* PROC SQL creates a new table that contains two new columns of summary data, REGTOTAL and REGPCT. Because the data are grouped by REGION, the summary SUM function sums data in each group, not the entire table. Thus, to get the total for each region, simply use the SUM function on the AMOUNT column. The region total becomes the values of the REGTOTAL column. To calculate a percentage for each REPID, divide AMOUNT by the sum of AMOUNT for the region and multiply by 100. The percentage of the total becomes the values of the REGPCT column:

```
proc sql;
   create table percent2 as
       select *, sum(amount) as regtotal format=dollar10.,
              100*(amount/sum(amount)) as regpct format=6.2
           from sales
           group by region;
quit;
```

Note: In PROC SQL, SELECT *statements* automatically produce a report. SELECT *clauses*, which follow CREATE TABLE or CREATE VIEW statements, do not automatically produce a report.

---

*   A PROC SQL table is a SAS data set. In SQL terminology, columns are variables and rows are observations.

Example 5.11

Adding a New Variable that Contains the Frequency of a BY-Group Value

Goal

For each row in a table, determine the number of occurrences of a column's value, and store the number in a new column.*

Strategy

Use the COUNT function in the SQL procedure to obtain a frequency count. Create a new table that includes a column that shows the frequency count. Use the GROUP BY clause so that the frequency count will be for each group.

Input Data Set

ONE

OBS	ID	NAME	LOCATION	HOURS
1	1	John Krueger	Tech Support	5
2	2	Joe Olszweski	Marketing	3
3	1	John Krueger	Tech Support	10
4	3	Len Nuhn	Sales	30
5	3	Len Nuhn	Sales	1
6	2	Joe Olszweski	Marketing	20
7	1	John Krueger	Tech Support	30
8	1	John Krueger	Tech Support	40
9	4	Luan Nguyen	Development	40

Resulting Data Set

Output 5.11   FINAL Table

FINAL

OBS	ID	NAME	LOCATION	HOURS	COUNT
1	1	John Krueger	Tech Support	30	4
2	1	John Krueger	Tech Support	10	4
3	1	John Krueger	Tech Support	5	4
4	1	John Krueger	Tech Support	40	4
5	2	Joe Olszweski	Marketing	20	2
6	2	Joe Olszweski	Marketing	3	2
7	3	Len Nuhn	Sales	1	2
8	3	Len Nuhn	Sales	30	2
9	4	Luan Nguyen	Development	40	1

---

*   A PROC SQL table is a SAS data set. In SQL terminology, columns are variables and rows are observations.

Program

The objective is to create a new table that shows how many times each employee appears in the original table. Group the data by values of ID. Count the number of rows in each group. Create a new column that shows how many times the employee appears in the original table:

Invoke PROC SQL, and create a table. The CREATE TABLE statement creates the table FINAL to store the results of the subsequent query.

```
proc sql;
   create table final as
```

Select the columns. The SELECT clause selects all columns from table ONE and creates an additional column, COUNT. For each row, the COUNT function uses the row's value of ID to return a frequency count that shows the total number of rows that have the same value of ID.

```
      select *, count(id) as count
```

Name the table to query.

```
      from one
```

Group the data by values of ID. Because the values are grouped by ID, the COUNT function will return the total number of rows for each value of ID. Without the GROUP BY clause, the COUNT function returns the total number of rows in the table.

```
      group by id;
quit;
```

Note: In PROC SQL, SELECT *statements* automatically produce a report. SELECT *clauses,* which follow CREATE TABLE or CREATE VIEW statements, do not automatically produce a report.

Example 5.12

Subsetting a Data Set Based on the Calculated Average of a BY Group

Goal

Group the data in a table* and create a new column that contains an average for each group. Use the average for each group to subset the table.

Strategy

Using the SQL procedure, create a new table that contains a column that gives the average of values from a specified column. Use the GROUP BY clause to group the data and find the average for each group. Use the HAVING clause to subset the table and to return only rows from each group that meet a specific search criterion.

Input Data Set

EMPLOYEE

OBS	NAME	JOBCODE	SALARY
1	Nikos	A1	$32,456.00
2	Paul	NA2	$53,798.00
3	Jody	T2	$25,147.00
4	Olga	T1	$19,810.00
5	Yao	NA1	$43,433.00
6	Natasha	A1	$31,987.00
7	Tom	T2	$23,596.00
8	Kendrick	NA1	$41,690.00
9	Kesha	A1	$33,067.00
10	Klaus	T1	$22,230.00
11	Kyle	NA2	$51,081.00
12	Carla	NA2	$52,270.00
13	Anne	T2	$24,876.00
14	Gunner	NA1	$42,345.00
15	Candice	A1	$34,567.00

Resulting Data Set

Output 5.12 FINAL Table

FINAL

OBS	NAME	JOBCODE	SALARY	AVERAGE
1	Kesha	A1	$33,067.00	$33,019.25
2	Candice	A1	$34,567.00	$33,019.25
3	Yao	NA1	$43,433.00	$42,489.33
4	Paul	NA2	$53,798.00	$52,383.00
5	Klaus	T1	$20,230.00	$20,020.00
6	Anne	T2	$24,876.00	$24,539.67
7	Jody	T2	$25,147.00	$24,539.67

---

* A PROC SQL table is a SAS data set. In SQL terminology, columns are variables and rows are observations.

Program

The objective is to find which employees make higher salaries than the average salary for their jobcode. Calculate the average salary for each jobcode and create a new column that contains the average. Use the average salary for each jobcode and each employee's salary to subset the table:

Invoke PROC SQL, and create a table. The CREATE TABLE statement creates the table FINAL to store the results of the subsequent query.

Select the columns. The SELECT clause selects all the columns from EMPLOYEE and creates an additional column, AVERAGE. The AVG function calculates the average for all the values of SALARY for each JOBCODE, which becomes the value of AVERAGE.

Name the table to query.

Group the data by JOBCODE, and subset the grouped data. GROUP BY specifies that AVERAGE will contain the average salary for each JOBCODE. The HAVING clause returns all rows where the employee's salary is greater than the average for their jobcode. CALCULATED takes the place of the mathematical computation in the SELECT clause. (HAVING requires that the data be grouped.)

```
proc sql;
   create table final as



      select *, avg(salary) as average format=dollar10.2






         from employee

         group by jobcode
         having salary >calculated average;
quit;
```

Note: In PROC SQL, SELECT *statements* automatically produce a report. SELECT *clauses*, which follow CREATE TABLE or CREATE VIEW statements, do not automatically produce a report.

Example 5.13

Really Rounding Numbers

Goal

Produce pencil-and-paper results* when rounding the results of numeric calculations.

Strategy

Introduce a *fuzz factor*** that allows you to obtain numeric calculations that are closer to the pencil-and-paper results that you expect. In a macro, use the regular ROUND function, but first add a fuzz factor to the number.

🔍   Due to factors of numeric precision, the ROUND function without an added fuzz factor does not always produce pencil-and-paper results. See "A Closer Look."

Input Data Set

AMT2 contains the pencil-and-paper rounded version of the number in AMT1 and is in the data set so that we can compare it against the results of a rounding technique.

	AMOUNTS	
OBS	AMT1	AMT2
1	0.0000540	0.0000500
2	0.0000550	0.0000600
3	0.0000560	0.0000600
4	0.9998050	0.9998100
5	0.9998060	0.9998100
6	17.9998050	17.9998100
7	17.9998060	17.9998100
8	18.9998050	18.9998100
9	18.9998060	18.9998100
10	18.9999050	18.9999100
11	18.9999060	18.9999100

Resulting Data Sets

Output 5.13a   MACRND Data Set

MACRND shows rounding with a fuzz factor.

		MACRND		
OBS	AMT1	AMT2	M_ROUND	MATCH
1	0.000054	0.000050	0.000050	yes
2	0.000055	0.000060	0.000060	yes
3	0.000056	0.000060	0.000060	yes
4	0.999805	0.999810	0.999810	yes
5	0.999806	0.999810	0.999810	yes
6	17.999805	17.999810	17.999810	yes
7	17.999806	17.999810	17.999810	yes
8	18.999805	18.999810	18.999810	yes
9	18.999806	18.999810	18.999810	yes
10	18.999905	18.999910	18.999910	yes
11	18.999906	18.999910	18.999910	yes

---

*   *Pencil-and-paper* results are produced by manual calculations.
**   *Fuzz factor* refers to adding an amount to a value so that it is rounded up appropriately when calculations are performed.

Output 5.13b REGRND Data Set

REGRND shows rounding with the
ROUND Function and no fuzzing.

		REGRND		
OBS	AMT1	AMT2	R_ROUND	MATCH
1	0.000054	0.000050	0.000050	yes
2	0.000055	0.000060	0.000060	yes
3	0.000056	0.000060	0.000060	yes
4	0.999805	0.999810	0.999810	yes
5	0.999806	0.999810	0.999810	yes
6	17.999805	17.999810	17.999800	no
7	17.999806	17.999810	17.999810	yes
8	18.999805	18.999810	18.999800	no
9	18.999806	18.999810	18.999810	yes
10	18.999905	18.999910	18.999900	no
11	18.999906	18.999910	18.999910	yes

Program

The objective is to produce rounded values that are the same as
pencil-and-paper results. The program uses a macro to introduce a fuzzing
factor when rounding a value. For comparison purposes, data set AMOUNTS
contains the variable AMT2, whose value is the correct pencil-and-paper
rounded value of AMT1. The program rounds AMT1 with a macro, produces
M_ROUND, and then compares its value with AMT2. The TEST is set to
'YES' when the values match so that you can easily see the result of
fuzz-factor rounding:

■ *Create the MACROUND macro.*

```
%macro macround(var,unit,fuzz=1e-10);
   round ((&var+(sign(&var)*&fuzz)),&unit)
%mend;
```

*Create MACRND. Read an observation
from AMOUNTS.*

```
data macrnd;
   format amt1 amt2 m_round 10.6;
   set amounts;
```

■ *Use the MACROUND macro to round
the value of AMT1 to six decimal places.
Assign the value to M_ROUND.*

```
   m_round=%macround(amt1,.00001);
```

*To show how well the rounding worked,
test the pencil-and-paper value in AMT2
against M_ROUND for a match.*

```
   if amt2=m_round then match='yes';
   else match='no';
run;
```

■ A Closer Look

■ Numeric Precision and the ROUND Function

We are introducing a fuzz factor because of a numeric precision problem
common to computer applications, not because the ROUND function produces
inaccurate results. The problem of numeric precision arises because of
hardware limitations in the way computers store real numbers. Basically, a
finite set of numbers must be used to represent the infinite real number system.

Most software packages and spreadsheet applications introduce a hidden fuzz
factor to account for problems in numeric precision. The SAS ROUND
function, however, does not use an automatic fuzzing mechanism. It simply
accepts the *original* value as it had been stored on the machine. Unless you add
this fuzz factor, however, numeric precision may prevent you from achieving

the usual pencil-and-paper results. Numeric precision is an issue across *all* platforms and is not consistent from machine to machine.

The key to defining your own rounding routine is to determine how much of a fuzz factor should be added. You want to add enough so that values are rounded up when they should be, but you do not want to add so much that values that should be rounded down are also rounded up instead. See "The MACROUND Macro and the Fuzz Factor" for a discussion of the rounding routine used in this program.

So that you can compare the results, the following program is the same as the original one *except* that it uses the ROUND function with no fuzzing factor:

```
data regrnd;
   format amt1 amt2 r_round 10.6;
   set amounts;
   r_round=round(amt1,.00001);
   if amt2=r_round then match='yes';
   else match='no';
run;
```

Output 5.13b shows that the rounded numbers in REGRND do not match the pencil-and-paper answers as well as the MACRND values do in Output 5.13a.

◙ The MACROUND Macro and the Fuzz Factor

The MACROUND macro uses the ROUND function with an additional fuzz factor to produce pencil-and-paper results when rounding a number. When the macro is defined, macro parameters in the %MACRO statement define three macro variables: VAR, UNIT, and FUZZ. The variable FUZZ is assigned a value at that time.

```
%macro macround(var,unit,fuzz=1e-10);
   round ((&var+(sign(&var)*&fuzz)),&unit)
%mend;
```

When you invoke the MACROUND macro, values for VAR and UNIT are supplied:

```
m_round=%macround(amt1,.00001);
```

At macro execution time, the macro variables are resolved:

```
m_round=round((amt1+(sign(amt1)*(1e-10))),.00001)
```

The routine used here ensures that a value that should be rounded up will be rounded correctly, even when its value was slightly less because of the representation error. The SIGN function is important here because it ensures that negative values are rounded in the correct direction. The SIGN function returns a negative value when AMT1 is negative. Without it, a negative value for AMT1 would be rounded in the wrong direction.

As an example, here's how the expression works when it executes for the first observation in this example:

```
m_round=round(0.000054+(sign(0.000054)*(1e-10)),.00001)
m_round=round(0.000054+.0000000001,.00001)
m_round=round(0.0000540001,.00001)
m_round=.000050
```

Where to Go from Here

□ **Numeric precision.** For a discussion of this issue, see pp. 88–95 in *SAS Language: Reference, Version 6, First Edition.* For more discussion, see Klenz, Brad (1992), "Handling Numeric Representation Error in SAS Applications," *Observations,* 1(3), 19–30.

□ **Macro processing.** For useful introductions, see Chapter 1, "Introducing the Macro Facility," in *SAS Macro Facility Tips and Techniques.* For complete reference information, see *SAS Guide to Macro Processing, Version 6, First Edition.*

Example 5.14

Collapsing Observations within a BY Group into a Single Observation

Goal

Rearrange a data set by changing a single variable in a group of observations to a group of variables in one observation. Reshape data by collapsing observations within a BY group into a single observation in order to simplify data analysis and report generation.

Strategy

Collapse multiple observations with a common BY variable value into a single observation. The data set must be sorted prior to the DATA step. Use a BY statement to create BY groups and the FIRST.*variable* and LAST.*variable*. Use array processing to assign the current value of a certain variable to the appropriate new variable. Use the FIRST.*variable* to control a DO loop that reinitializes the retained array values and resets the array subscript variable. Use the LAST.*variable* to output the newly created observation.

Input Data Sets

STUDENTS has duplicate values for the BY variable NAME and may contain up to three observations for each value of NAME.

STUDENTS

OBS	NAME	SCORE
1	Deborah	89
2	Deborah	90
3	Deborah	95
4	Martin	90
5	Stefan	89
6	Stefan	76

Resulting Data Set

Output 5.14 SCORES Data Set

SCORES

OBS	NAME	SCORE1	SCORE2	SCORE3
1	Deborah	89	90	95
2	Martin	90	.	.
3	Stefan	89	76	.

Program

Each observation in the data set STUDENTS currently stores a single score. The objective is to reshape STUDENTS so that an observation contains all test scores for an individual student. Use array processing to create and assign values to the new variables SCORE1, SCORE2, and SCORE3. The values are retained with each iteration of the DATA step, and the record is written only when the last observation in the BY group is processed. This program assumes that STUDENTS contains no more than three observations with the same value for NAME:

Create SCORES. Use the RETAIN statement to create the variables SCORE1–SCORE3 and to retain the values of NAME and SCORE1–SCORE3 from one iteration of the DATA step to the next.

```
data scores(keep=name score1-score3);
   retain name score1-score3;
```

Create the array SCORES. SCORE1–SCORE3 will receive their values from the variable SCORE in STUDENTS.

```
   array scores(*) score1-score3;
```

Read observations from STUDENTS. Use the BY statement to create BY groups and the variables FIRST.NAME and LAST.NAME.

```
   set students;
   by name;
```

At the beginning of each BY group, use the assignment statement to set the value of the array subscript I to 1. Reinitialize to missing the values of SCORE1–SCORE3.

```
   if first.name then do;
      i=1;
      do j=1 to 3;
         scores(j)=.;
      end;
   end;
```

Assign the current value of SCORE to SCORE1, SCORE2, or SCORE3.

```
   scores(i)=score;
```

After processing the last observation in a BY group, write an observation to SCORES.

```
   if last.name then output;
```

Increase the value of I by 1. In addition to increasing the value, the sum statement also causes it to be automatically retained across iterations of the DATA step.

```
   i+1;
run;
```

Example 5.15

Expanding Single Observations into Multiple Observations

Goal

Reshape data by creating multiple observations from a single observation in the input data set and by assigning variable names as values in the output data set.

Strategy

Use an array and a DO loop to create multiple observations from each single observation in the input data set. Use the CALL routine VNAME to assign variable names from the input data set as values of a new variable in the output data set.

Input Data Set

SURVEY

OBS	NAME	CEREAL	PASTRY	BAGEL
1	John	10	9	8
2	Sam	2	8	4
3	Sally	5	7	6

Resulting Data Set

Output 5.15   SURVEY2 Data Set

SURVEY2 contains reshaped survey data.

SURVEY2

OBS	NAME	BREAKFST	RESPONSE
1	John	CEREAL	10
2	John	PASTRY	9
3	John	BAGEL	8
4	Sam	CEREAL	2
5	Sam	PASTRY	8
6	Sam	BAGEL	4
7	Sally	CEREAL	5
8	Sally	PASTRY	7
9	Sally	BAGEL	6

Program

The objective is to read SURVEY and create a new data set in which the variable names CEREAL, PASTRY, and BAGEL become values for the new variable BREAKFST and in which three observations are created for each one in SURVEY. The numeric values of the variables CEREAL, PASTRY, and BAGEL are written to the new variable RESPONSE:

Create SURVEY2, dropping the variables whose values are being written to the new variable RESPONSE and dropping the variable used by the iterative DO loop. Read an observation from SURVEY.

```
data survey2(drop=cereal pastry bagel i);
    set survey;
```

Define the array NUM. Define character variable BREAKFST and give it a length of eight.

```
    array num (*) cereal pastry bagel;
    length breakfst $ 8;
```

Assign values to RESPONSE and BREAKFST. Write an observation to SURVEY2 each time the DO loop iterates. This DO loop iterates three times, once for each element in the array. In each loop, the assignment statement uses the NUM array to write the numeric value of either CEREAL, PASTRY, or BAGEL to the new numeric variable RESPONSE. The CALL routine VNAME assigns the name of that variable (CEREAL, PASTRY, or BAGEL) to BREAKFST.

```
    do i=1 to dim(num);
        response=num[i];
        call vname(num[i],breakfst);
        output;
    end;
run;
```

Example 5.16

Reshaping Observations into Multiple Variables

Goal

Transpose* a data set to make the information more meaningful and usable for further processing. The process of transposing is repeated until the final goal is met.

Strategy

Sometimes data that are stored as numerical values actually have greater significance and potential usability than is apparent. To improve meaning and usability, use a multi-step process to transpose a data set so that information originally stored in a few numeric variables with numerous observations is stored as multiple variables with fewer observations.

First, use the TRANSPOSE procedure with the VAR statement to reshape the variable so that its values are stored in a series of new variables. Use one variable as a BY variable to create one observation for each unique value of that variable. Write the results to an output data set.

Second, transpose all of the variables in the output data set so that each variable name is now a value of a new character variable. Store the values of each variable in another series of variables and create a new output data set.

Input Data Set

ONE

OBS	CATEGORY	RATING
1	1	6
2	1	9
3	1	8
4	1	9
5	1	8
6	1	10
7	1	10
8	2	7
9	2	8
10	2	8
11	2	10
12	2	9
13	2	8
14	2	10
15	3	6
16	3	9
17	3	9
18	3	9
19	3	8
20	3	9
21	3	9

---

* To *transpose* is to reshape data by turning columns (variables) of information into rows (observations).

Resulting Data Sets

Output 5.16a INTERIM, First Transposed Data Set

```
                                   INTERIM

     OBS    FORD    NISSAN    MAZDA    SAAB    SATURN    HONDA    TOYOTA

      1      6        9         8        9        8        10       10
      2      7        8         8       10        9         8       10
      3      6        9         9        9        8         9        9
```

Output 5.16b FINAL, Final Transposed Data Set

```
                          FINAL

     OBS    MAKE     DEPEND    APPEAL    PERFORM

      1    FORD        6         7         6
      2    NISSAN      9         8         9
      3    MAZDA       8         8         9
      4    SAAB        9        10         9
      5    SATURN      8         9         8
      6    HONDA      10         8         9
      7    TOYOTA     10        10         9
```

Program

The data set ONE contains survey data that have been collected on the dependability, overall appeal, and performance of cars from seven manufacturers. However, the results are stored simply as values in the numeric variables CATEGORY and RATING. Not only are the data not useful in their current form for further processing, but their meaning is actually *buried*.

Reshape the values in a two-step process to reflect their real meaning and to make the data usable. In the first step, transpose RATING so its values are stored in a series of new variables, each reflecting a car manufacturer. Do not transpose the values of CATEGORY. Simply *collapse* the values into one observation corresponding to each BY group. The resulting data set INTERIM has seven variables, one for each car manufacturer, and three observations.

In the second step, transpose the seven car variables so that each variable name is now the value of a new variable, MAKE. Store the values of each car variable in the three new variables DEPEND, APPEAL, and PERFORM, which reflect the qualities surveyed. The resulting data set, FINAL, has four variables, one for the make of car and three reflecting the three qualities. It has seven observations.

Create INTERIM by reshaping ONE.
Transpose the variable RATING. Use
CATEGORY as a BY variable to create an
observation for each unique value of
CATEGORY. The INTERIM data set will
have three observations; the BY statement
used with PROC TRANSPOSE generates a
single observation for each BY group of
CATEGORY. The VAR statement specifies
that only the variable RATING is to be
transposed. The variables COL1–COL7 are
created automatically to contain the values
of RATING from every observation of the
BY group. _NAME_ is created
automatically to specify the name of the
variable being transposed. Because it is
unneeded, it is dropped.

```
proc transpose data=one
               out=interim(drop=_name_ category
                           rename=(col1=Ford col2=Nissan col3=Mazda
                                   col4=Saab col5=Saturn
                                   col6=Honda col7=Toyota));
   by category;
   var rating;
run;
```

Create FINAL by reshaping INTERIM,
this time transposing all of the variables.
Without a VAR statement or another
statement, the seven numeric variables,
FORD–TOYOTA, are all transposed.
NAME is created automatically; its
values are the names of the transposed
variables FORD–TOYOTA. The variables
COL1–COL3 are created automatically to
contain values for the three qualities.
NAME and COL1–COL3 are renamed
appropriately.

```
proc transpose data=interim
               out=final(rename=(_name_=make col1=depend
                                 col2=appeal col3=perform));
run;
```

CHAPTER 6
Utilities and Functions

This chapter is not strictly about combining observations from different SAS data sets. It contains, however, examples of commonly asked questions about dealing with data values, such as extracting character strings from a variable value, converting a numeric variable to a character variable and vice versa, performing a bubble sort, and determining someone's age from a SAS date value, among others.

Example 6.1

Converting Variable Types from Character to Numeric and Vice Versa

Goal

Read the value of a character variable and write its value to a numeric variable, and vice versa.

Strategy

You cannot directly change the type of a variable. You must create a new variable of the desired type. Use the PUT or INPUT function and a specified format or informat, respectively, to convert a value. Use an assignment statement to assign that value to the new variable. When converting character to numeric, use the INPUT function and a numeric informat. To do the reverse, use the PUT function and a numeric format.

Input Data Sets

Data set ONE contains a single character variable. Data set TWO contains a single numeric variable.

	ONE		TWO
OBS	XCHAR	OBS	YNUM
1	0123	1	123
2	12345	2	12345
3	123456	3	999
4	123A45	4	.

Resulting Data Sets

Output 6.1a   CHAR2NUM Data Set

		CHAR2NUM	
OBS	XCHAR	XNUM
1	0123	123
2	12345	12345
3	123456	123456
4	123A45	.

Output 6.1b   NUM2CHAR Data Set

		NUM2CHAR	
OBS	YNUM	YCHAR1	YCHAR2
1	123	000123	123
2	12345	012345	12345
3	999	000999	999
4	.		.

Output 6.1c   CHAR2NM2 Data Set

	CHAR2NM2
OBS	XCHAR
1	123
2	12345
3	123456
4	.

Program

The objective is to read a character value and write it, if possible, as a numeric value to a new variable, or vice versa. To write the character value of XCHAR to the numeric variable XNUM, use the INPUT function to return the existing character value as it is read with the numeric informat 8. To write the value of numeric variable YNUM as a value for character variables YCHAR1 and YCHAR2, use the PUT function and the numeric format Z6. to return the existing numeric value with leading zeros, or use the PUT function with the standard numeric format 6. to return the numeric value without leading zeros. In all three cases, use an assignment statement to save the returned value to the new variable XNUM, YCHAR1, or YCHAR2, respectively:

Create CHAR2NUM. Read an observation from ONE.

```
data char2num;
   set one;

   xnum = input(xchar,?? 8.);
run;
```

Read the value of XCHAR with a numeric informat and assign it as a numeric value to XNUM, a numeric variable. The INPUT function reads the value of XCHAR with the numeric informat 8. and returns a numeric value. The ?? format modifier suppresses the invalid data messages and prevents the automatic variable _ERROR_ from being set to 1 if XCHAR doesn't contain valid numeric data.

Create NUM2CHAR. Read an observation from TWO.

```
data num2char;
   set two;

   ychar1 = put(ynum,z6.);
   ychar2 = put(ynum, 6.);
```

Assign values to YCHAR1 and YCHAR2 by formatting the current value of YNUM with the formats Z6. and 6., respectively. The PUT function writes the current value of the specified variable with the specified format. The format Z6. formats the value of YNUM with leading zeros. The format 6. is the standard numeric format.

If the value for YNUM is missing, then explicitly assign YCHAR1 a value of blank. Assigning a blank to YCHAR1 overrides the default value of a period (for missing).

```
   if ynum=. then ychar1=' ';
run;
```

Related Technique

You can drop and rename variables so that the new variable with the numeric value can retain the same name as the original variable it was created from:

```
data char2nm2(drop=x);
   set one(rename=(xchar=x));
   xchar = input(x,?? 8.);
run;
```

See Output 6.1c.

Example 6.2

Determining the Type of a Variable's Content

Goal

Determine whether a character variable's value contains numeric data, character data, or missing data.

Strategy

To determine the contents of a character variable's value for each observation, first test the value to see if it is missing (blank). If it is missing, classify it as undefined. If it is not missing, then use the INPUT function to read the value with a numeric format. If that result is not missing, it is a valid numeric value. If it is missing, it is classified as a character value.

Input Data Sets

OLD contains character variable X.

```
OLD

OBS    X

 1     1234
 2     12E5
 3
 4     124ABC
 5     124
 6     ABCDEFGH
```

Resulting Data Set

Output 6.2 NEW Data Set

```
              NEW

OBS    TYPE        X

 1     Numeric     1234
 2     Numeric     12E5
 3     Undefined
 4     Character   124ABC
 5     Numeric     124
 6     Character   ABCDEFGH
```

Program

The objective is to determine the data type of the value of variable X in each observation in data set OLD. Read each observation and test to see if the value of X is missing (blank). If it is missing, set a new variable named TYPE to "Undefined". For all other observations, assign a value to a temporary variable by using the INPUT function and a numeric informat to return a numeric value. If the value is not missing, it is a valid numeric value. If it is missing, it is a character value.

Create NEW. Read an observation from OLD. The LENGTH function assigns a length of 9 to the new character variable TYPE. By default, TYPE would have been created with a length of 8.

```
data new(drop=tempvar);
   length type $ 9.;
   set old;
```

If the value of X is blank, it is neither character nor numeric so set TYPE appropriately. There is no need to do further checking, so return to the top of the DATA step.

```
   if x=' ' then
      do;
         type='Undefined';
         return;
      end;
```

Create variable TEMPVAR and assign it a value by using the INPUT function to return the value of X read with the numeric format 8. If the value is not missing, assign a value to TYPE that indicates that it is numeric. Otherwise, indicate that it is character. The INPUT function converts the character values to numeric values. The ?? format modifier suppresses the invalid data messages and prevents the automatic variable _ERROR_ from being set to 1 when invalid data are read.

```
   tempvar=input(x,?? 8.);
   if tempvar ne . then
      type = 'Numeric';
   else
      type = 'Character';
run;
```

Example 6.3

Determining Whether a Variable is Character or Numeric

Goal

Determine if a variable is character or numeric to ensure that you have the right type of data for your application.

Strategy

Query the table* DICTIONARY.COLUMNS in PROC SQL to determine the variable's type. Use the INTO clause to store the variable's type in a macro variable. Use the macro variable in a subsequent DATA step to create a new variable of the other type that contains the same data as the original variable.

Input Data Set

Data set ONE contains two variables: the numeric variable X_NUM and the character variable Y_CHAR.

```
               ONE

    OBS     X_NUM    Y_CHAR

     1      12345    12345
```

Resulting Data Sets

Output 6.3a   NUM2CHAR Data Set

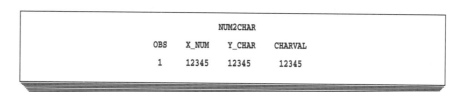

```
                      NUM2CHAR

         OBS    X_NUM    Y_CHAR    CHARVAL
          1     12345    12345     12345
```

Output 6.3b   CHAR2NUM Data Set

```
                      CHAR2NUM

         OBS    X_NUM    Y_CHAR    NUMVAL
          1     12345    12345     12345
```

Program

The objective is to ensure that you are using a certain type of data in your application.

The table DICTIONARY.COLUMNS contains information about all variables in all SAS data sets in the current SAS session. For each variable in data set ONE, query DICTIONARY.COLUMNS to determine its type. You must subset the query to get the type for only one variable. (Typically, you subset queries of dictionary tables with a WHERE clause because they are very large

---

*   A PROC SQL table is a SAS data set. In SQL terminology, columns are variables and rows are observations.

tables.) The query returns the value **num** or the value **char**. Store the value in a macro variable. Use the macro variable in a subsequent DATA step. The DATA step creates a new data set and a new variable that contains the same data as the original variable, but of a different type.

In many cases, SAS automatically changes data from one type to another, but it is more efficient if you do it. In addition, if you control the conversion, you can avoid possible unexpected results when numeric data defaults to using the BEST12. format.

Query DICTIONARY.COLUMNS to learn the type of X_NUM. The column TYPE in DICTIONARY.COLUMNS contains the variable type for all variables active in the current SAS session. The INTO clause puts the value **num** in the macro variable VARTYPE.

```
proc sql;
   select type into : vartype
      from dictionary.columns
```

Subset the query. To get the type for only X_NUM, subset the query to return only the row for that variable. The values in the dictionary table are in upper case, so the WHERE clause must use upper case as well.

```
      where libname='WORK' and
            memname='ONE' and
            name='X_NUM';
quit;
```

Create a new data set and a new variable that contains the same data as the original variable, but of a different type. The PUT function returns the value of X_NUM as character data. The character data is stored in the variable CHARVAL. The value **num** for VARTYPE is lower case, so the IF statement must use lower case as well.

```
data num2char;
   set one;
   if "&vartype"="num" then charval=put(x_num,5.);
run;
```

Query DICTIONARY.COLUMNS to learn the type of Y_CHAR. The column TYPE in DICTIONARY.COLUMNS contains the variable type for all variables active in the current SAS session. The INTO clause puts the value **char** in the macro variable VARTYPE.

```
proc sql;
   select type into : vartype
      from dictionary.columns
```

Subset the query. To get the type for only Y_CHAR, subset the query to return only the row for that variable.

```
      where libname='WORK' and
            memname='ONE' and
            name='Y_CHAR';
quit;
```

Create a new data set and a new variable that contains the same data as the original variable but of a different type. The INPUT function returns the value of Y_CHAR as numeric. The numeric value is stored in the variable NUMVAL.

```
data char2num;
   set one;
   if "&vartype"="char" then numval=input(y_char,5.);
run;
```

Note: In PROC SQL, SELECT *statements* automatically produce a report. SELECT *clauses*, which follow CREATE TABLE or CREATE VIEW statements, do not automatically produce a report.

Where to Go from Here

□ **Dictionary tables.**

  □ For an example that describes dictionary tables more thoroughly, see Example 6.4, "Creating a SAS Data Set Whose Variables Contain the Attributes of Variables from Another Data Set," in this book.

  □ For a complete description and examples of dictionary tables, see pp. 286–291 and pp. 294–295 in Chapter 37, "The SQL Procedure," in SAS Technical Report P-222, *Changes and Enhancements to Base SAS Software, Release 6.07*.

  □ For examples that use dictionary tables, see Chapter 11, "Five Nifty Reports Using PROC SQL Views in the SASHELP Library" by Bernadette Johnson in *Reporting from the Field: SAS Software Experts Present Real-World Report-Writing Applications*.

Example 6.4

Creating a SAS Data Set Whose Variables Contain the Attributes of Variables from Another SAS Data Set

Goal

Create a table* that has information about the name, type, and length of columns in another table.

Strategy

PROC SQL provides *dictionary tables*, which contain information about the SAS files in the current SAS session. Dictionary tables are accessed by the predefined libref DICTIONARY. Dictionary tables are no different from other PROC SQL tables, except that the information in them is gathered and maintained by the SAS System.

The table DICTIONARY.COLUMNS contains information about all of the columns in all the tables in the current SAS session. Use the DESCRIBE TABLE statement on the DICTIONARY.COLUMNS table to determine the column names that you need in your query.

CAUTION!

Because DICTIONARY.COLUMNS is usually a very large table, use a WHERE clause to restrict the query to only one table. ■

Input Data Set

			PRICES				
OBS	CROP	MARKET	HIGH	LOW	LAST	MONTH
1	Wheat	Farmville	2.96	2.64	2.7	jul94

Resulting SAS Log

Output 6.4a Columns in DICTIONARY.COLUMNS

The descriptions of the columns used in this example are shaded.

```
NOTE: SQL table DICTIONARY.COLUMNS was created like:

create table DICTIONARY.COLUMNS
   (
   LIBNAME char(8) label='Library Name',
   MEMNAME char(8) label='Member Name',
   MEMTYPE char(8) label='Member Type',
   NAME char(8) label='Column Name',
   TYPE char(4) label='Column Type',
   LENGTH num label='Column Length',
   NPOS num label='Column Position',
   VARNUM num label='Column Number in Table',
   LABEL char(40) label='Column Label',
   FORMAT char(16) label='Column Format',
   INFORMAT char(16) label='Column Informat',
   IDXUSAGE char(9) label='Column Index Type'
   );
```

---

*   A PROC SQL table is a SAS data set. In SQL terminology, columns are variables and rows are observations.

Resulting Data Set

Output 6.4b   ATTR Table

```
                            ATTR

              Column    Column    Column
      OBS      Type      Name     Length

       1       char      MONTH       5
       2       char      CROP        5
       3       char      MARKET      9
       4       num       LAST        8
       5       num       LOW         8
       6       num       HIGH        8
```

Program

Look at your SAS log to determine that you need to use the TYPE, NAME, and LENGTH columns from DICTIONARY.COLUMNS to get the type, name, and length of variables in WORK.PRICES. In addition, use the LIBNAME and MEMNAME columns to subset DICTIONARY.COLUMNS to produce information about the columns in WORK.PRICES, only. Lastly, order the table so that the character columns and the numeric columns are listed together:

Invoke PROC SQL and determine the column names in DICTIONARY.COLUMNS. The DESCRIBE TABLE statement writes a description of the table to the SAS log.

```
proc sql;
    describe table dictionary.columns;
```

Create a table. The CREATE TABLE statement creates the table ATTR to store the results of the subsequent query.

```
    create table attr as
```

Select the appropriate columns.

```
      select type, name, length
```

Name the dictionary table to query. You do not have to assign the libref DICTIONARY.

```
      from dictionary.columns
```

Subset the query. The values of LIBNAME and MEMNAME must be uppercase.

```
      where libname='WORK' and memname='PRICES'
```

Order the data values by variable type.

```
      order by type;
quit;
```

Note: In PROC SQL, SELECT *statements* automatically produce a report. SELECT *clauses*, which follow CREATE TABLE or CREATE VIEW statements, do not automatically produce a report.

Where to Go from Here

□ **Dictionary tables.** For a complete description and examples of dictionary tables, see pp. 286–291 and pp. 294–295 in Chapter 37, "The SQL Procedure," in SAS Technical Report P-222, *Changes and Enhancements to Base SAS Software, Release 6.07.*

For examples that use dictionary tables, see Chapter 11, "Five Nifty Reports Using PROC SQL Views in the SASHELP Library" by Bernadette Johnson in *Reporting from the Field: SAS Software Experts Present Real-World Report-Writing Applications.*

Example 6.5

Sorting Variable Values within an Observation (Bubble Sort)

Goal

Sort the values of variables within an observation.

Strategy

To sort the values of variables within an observation, use a technique called *bubble sort*. Create an array that contains the variables that you want to sort. Then use nested DO UNTIL and iterative DO loops to compare the value of each variable in an observation with the next variable value until all have been compared and placed in ascending order.

For an enhanced version of this program that will increase efficiency for processing larger data sets, see "Related Technique."

Input Data Sets

ONE

OBS	CODE1	CODE2	CODE3	CODE4	CODE5	CODE6
1	3	1	5	4	6	2
2	9	8	6	5	7	4
3	3	2	1	9	0	7
4	8	2	6	4	0	1
5	5	7	4	3	8	2

Resulting Data Sets

Output 6.5a VARSORT Data Set

VARSORT

OBS	CODE1	CODE2	CODE3	CODE4	CODE5	CODE6
1	1	2	3	4	5	6
2	4	5	6	7	8	9
3	0	1	2	3	7	9
4	0	1	2	4	6	8
5	2	3	4	5	7	8

Output 6.5b VARSORT2 Data Set

VARSORT2 was produced by a technique shown in "Related Technique" that requires more coding but that is more efficient for larger data sets.

VARSORT2

OBS	CODE1	CODE2	CODE3	CODE4	CODE5	CODE6
1	1	2	3	4	5	6
2	4	5	6	7	8	9
3	0	1	2	3	7	9
4	0	1	2	4	6	8
5	2	3	4	5	7	8

Program

The objective is to reorder the values of CODE1 through CODE6 for each observation so that they are in ascending order. First, create the CODE array to contain the values for these six variables in each observation. Use a DO UNTIL loop that iterates until the data are completely sorted. Within that loop, nest an iterative DO loop that iterates five times, once for every comparison that needs to be made (CODE1 to CODE2, and so on). This DO loop makes the comparisons by processing the CODE array. Values are reordered if the next value in sequence is larger than its immediate predecessor.

Create VARSORT. Define array CODE. Read an observation from ONE.

```
data varsort(keep=code1-code6);
   array code(*) code1-code6;
   set one;
```

■ *Begin a DO UNTIL loop that iterates until all of the variable values within an observation have been sorted. Set SORTED to 1.* SORTED will be set to 0 each time the DO group executes to reorder values. When that code does not execute, the array is already sorted. In that case, SORTED will remain 1 and prevent the DO UNTIL loop from executing again.

```
   do until (sorted);
      sorted=1;
```

Begin an iterative DO loop that iterates five times, once for each comparison that needs to be made in each observation. The DIM function returns the number of elements in CODE (6). Using DIM prevents you from having to change the upper bound of an iterative DO group if you later change the number of array elements.

```
      do i = 1 to dim(code) 1;
```

Compare each value of an element in the CODE array (values of variables CODE1 through CODE6) with the value of the next variable. If the first element is larger, reorder the values and set SORTED to 0. The variable TEMP holds an array element while you assign the larger value to the second element and the smaller value to the first element. SORTED is set to 0 so that the DO UNTIL loop continues iterating. This DO group only executes when a value is greater than its immediate successor. After all values are in order, this block does not execute. SORTED is, therefore, not reset to 0, causing the DO UNTIL loop to stop.

```
         if code(i) > code(i+1) then
            do;
               temp=code(i+1);
               code(i+1)=code(i);
               code(i)=temp;
               sorted=0;
            end;
      end;
   end;
```

◨ A Closer Look

Processing the Array the Correct Number of Times

The key to processing the array the necessary number of times is in *where* the variable SORTED is set to 1. The value of SORTED controls the DO UNTIL loop that processes each observation. When SORTED is true (equal to 1), the DO UNTIL loop stops processing. SORTED is set to 1 *before* the code that reorders values. SORTED is set to 0 within the DO loop that reorders values. On the last time through, the reordering code never executes because the tested value is never greater than the following value. Because SORTED is not reset to 0 in that case, it equals 1 when the DO UNTIL statement executes and that ends the DO UNTIL loop. The entire DATA step iterates and another observation is read for processing.

Related Technique

If you are sorting a small data set, the technique described in "A Closer Look" is simple and useful. But if you are sorting a larger data set, the gain in efficiency can make it worth the effort to limit the comparisons performed to only those that are necessary. Set the upper bound of the iterative DO loop that compares values and switches them when necessary so that only pairs before the last pair switched are rechecked.

First, create two additional variables, HBND and MOVEHIGH in this example, that you can use to prevent the iterative DO loop from rechecking pairs unnecessarily. Use HBND to control how many times the DO loop that compares pairs of values iterates. Initially set HBND to the highest number necessary, the next-to-last element in the array. In the DO group that switches values when necessary, set the value of MOVEHIGH to I, the number of the iteration and, therefore, of the element in the array being processed. Use that value to reset the value of HBND. The next time the DO loop iterates, it will not check more pairs than are necessary:

```
data varsort2(keep=code1-code6);
   array code(*) code1-code6;
   set one;
   hbnd = dim(code)-1;
   do until (sorted);
      sorted=1;
      do i = 1 to hbnd;
         if code(i) > code(i+1) then
            do;
               temp=code(i+1);
               code(i+1)=code(i);
               code(i)=temp;
               movehigh=i;
               sorted=0;
            end;
      end;
      hbnd=movehigh-1;
   end;
run;
```

Example 6.6

Creating Equal-Sized Random Samples and Producing Equal-Sized Subsets or Exact-Sized Subsets

Goal

Create equal-sized subsets from randomly chosen observations from a data set. You can also create exact-sized subsets.

Note: You can create equal-sized subsets only if the number of observations is divisible by the number of subsets you want to create.

Strategy

Create a new version of the data set by adding a new variable whose values are randomly generated with the RANUNI function. Sort the new data set based on the values of that variable. Then read the sorted data set and calculate the value of a new variable for each observation, based on the remainder of the current value of _N_ divided by the number of subsets you want to create. Use conditional processing to write each observation to one of three data sets.

To create an exact-sized subset, simply use the OBS= data set option so that only a certain number of observations are read and then written to an output data set. See "Related Techniques."

Note: This technique is not efficient for large data sets. For more efficient sampling examples for larger data sets, see Chapter 10, "Processing Large Data Sets with SAS Software," in the *SAS Applications Guide, 1987 Edition.*

Input Data Sets

RANDOM was created by reading MASTER and using the RANUNI function to generate values for X. It is sorted by X.

	MASTER		RANDOM	
OBS	NAME	OBS	NAME	X
1	NCSU	1	Wake Forest	0.07789
2	Clemson	2	Maryland	0.18382
3	Georgia Tech	3	Duke	0.27628
4	Duke	4	NCSU	0.36292
5	Maryland	5	UNC	0.70725
6	Virginia	6	Virginia	0.72888
7	Wake Forest	7	Florida State	0.73432
8	Florida State	8	Clemson	0.74519
9	UNC	9	Georgia Tech	0.83106

Resulting Data Sets

Output 6.6a   ONE Data Set

```
                            ONE

              OBS    NAME

               1     Duke
               2     Virginia
               3     Georgia Tech
```

Output 6.6b   TWO Data Set

```
                            TWO

              OBS    NAME

               1     Wake Forest
               2     NCSU
               3     Florida State
```

Output 6.6c   THREE Data Set

```
                           THREE

              OBS    NAME

               1     Maryland
               2     UNC
               3     Clemson
```

Output 6.6d   SIMPLE Data Set

```
                           SIMPLE

              OBS    NAME

               1     Wake Forest
               2     Maryland
               3     Duke
               4     NCSU
               5     UNC
```

Program

The objective is to create three equal-sized subsets from the data set MASTER. In the DATA step, read each observation in MASTER and use the RANUNI function to generate random values of variable X between 0 and 1. Sort the data set by X. Use another DATA step to read the new data set RANDOM. Create the variable CLASS and calculate its value by using the MOD function to divide _N_ by 3 and return the remainder. Then use conditional processing to output each observation to a subset, based on the value of CLASS:

Create RANDOM. Read an observation from MASTER. Generate random numbers for variable X. The RANUNI function randomly generates numbers and returns a value based on the seed.

```
data random;
   set master;
   x=ranuni(12345);
run;
```

Sort RANDOM by X.

```
proc sort data=random;
   by x;
run;
```

Create data sets ONE, TWO, and THREE. Read an observation from RANDOM. Drop variables you do not need in the output data sets. Create the variable CLASS. The MOD function returns the remainder of _N_, the number of the current iteration, divided by 3, the number of subsets being created.

```
data one two three;
   set random;
   drop x class;
   class=mod(_N_,3);
```

Write an observation to ONE, TWO, or THREE, based on the value of CLASS.

```
   select (class);
      when (0) output one;
      when (1) output two;
      otherwise output three;
   end;
run;
```

Related Technique

To create a randomly selected subset of an exact size, use the OBS= data set option to read only a specific number of observations from RANDOM, in this case 5:

```
data simple(keep=name);
   set random(obs=5);
run;
```

See the resulting data set in Output 6.6d.

Example 6.7

Counting the Occurrences of a String within the Values of a Variable

Goal

Count the number of occurrences of a character string or of a single character in the value of a variable.

Strategy

First, use the TRANWRD function to substitute a single character for the search string in the variable value you're searching. Use COMPRESS to remove that character from the string and use the LENGTH function to check the length of the string both before and after the character has been removed. The difference in lengths indicates how many occurrences of the character string were in the original variable value.

Note: You must choose a substitute character that does not occur in your original character values.

Input Data Sets

Each value of MEMNAME contains one or more occurrences of the string **my**. The second observation contains the string **My** to demonstrate that the search is case sensitive.

```
                ONE

OBS    MEMNAME

 1     _my_lib_my
 2     _my_lib_My
 3     mylibmylibmylib
 4     my_libmylib_my
```

Resulting Data Sets

Output 6.7 TWO Data Set

The value of COUNT indicates the number of times **my** occurs in the value of MEMNAME.

```
                            TWO

OBS    MEMNAME          NEWMNAME         COUNT
 1     _my_lib_my       _&_lib_&           2
 2     _my_lib_My       _&_lib_My          1
 3     mylibmylibmylib  &lib&lib&lib       3
 4     my_libmylib_my   &_lib&lib_&        3
```

Program

Create TWO. Read an observation from ONE.

Determine how many times my occurs in MEMNAME. Change each instance of my in MEMNAME to &. Assign that value to NEWMNAME. Remove all ampersands (&) from NEWMNAME. Subtract the compressed length from the original length of NEWMNAME. Assign that value to COUNT. The TRANWRD function searches the current value of MEMNAME for my and changes each occurrence into an ampersand (&). The LENGTH function returns the length of a variable. The COMPRESS function removes all ampersands from NEWMNAME.

The objective is to count all occurrences of the string **my** in the values of MEMNAME in data set ONE. First, use the TRANWRD function to change all occurrences of **my** in each value of MEMNAME to an ampersand. Assign this value to a new variable, NEWMNAME. Use the COMPRESS function to remove all instances of **&** from the value of NEWMNAME. Use the LENGTH function to determine the length of NEWMNAME both with and without the compression. Assign this difference to COUNT, which indicates how many times **my** occurred in each value of MEMNAME:

```
data two;
   set one;

   newmname=tranwrd(memname,'my','&');
   count=length(newmname)-length(compress(newmname,'&'));
run;
```

Example 6.8

Extracting a Character String without Breaking the Text in the Middle of a Word

Goal

Extract from a variable a character string that is no longer than a specified length and that does not end in the middle of a word.

Strategy

Use the SUBSTR function and assignment statements to create two new variables from a character variable. One contains the character that would be last in the extracted string; the other contains the first character following the extracted string. If the last character or the first character following the string is a punctuation mark or a blank, assign the extracted string to a new variable. If not, use a DO loop to search backward in the string until a blank or punctuation mark is found, and then write to a variable the new, shorter string that does not end in the middle of a word.

Input Data Set

Variable COMMENTS contains a character value. The twenty-first character in each value contains either a blank, a punctuation mark, or a letter within a word.

```
                SURVEY

OBS             COMMENTS


 1    The food was served in a timely manner.
 2    The service was good!  Food was great!!
 3    The waiter was very helpful and courteous.
 4    My chicken is great, but service is slow!!!
 5    I love the restaurant!!! Service is great!!
```

Resulting Data Set

Output 6.8   NEW Data Set

```
                              NEW
     OBS              COMMENTS                    NEWCOMNT
      1    The food was served in a timely manner.    The food was served
      2    The service was good!  Food was great!!    The service was good
      3    The waiter was very helpful and courteou    The waiter was very
      4    My chicken is great, but service is slow    My chicken is great,
      5    I love the restaurant!!! Service is grea    I love the
```

Program

The objective is to create variable NEWCOMNT by extracting a character string from variable COMMENTS that is no longer than 20 characters and that does not end in the middle of a word. Use the SUBSTR function and an assignment statement to create two variables: NEXTCHAR consists of the twenty-first character, and CUTPT consists of the twentieth character. If NEXTCHAR or CUTPT is a blank or a punctuation mark, the string doesn't break in the middle of a word, so assign NEWCOMNT a value with the full 20 characters and write the observation. Otherwise, use an iterative DO loop to process NEWCOMNT again, on each iteration reading one less character and testing to see if it is a blank or a punctuation mark. When it is, assign NEWCOMNT a value whose length is determined by the iterative process, and write the observation with the new shorter value for NEWCOMNT:

Create NEW. Read an observation from SURVEY. Assign length of 20 to character variable NEWCOMNT.

```
data new(keep=comments newcomnt);
   set survey;
   length newcomnt $ 20;
```

Assign values to NEXTCHAR and CUTPT. The SUBSTR function reads a number of specified characters beginning at a specified location in variable COMMENTS.

```
   nextchar=substr(comments,21,1);
   cutpt=substr(comments,20,1);
```

Test variables CUTPT and NEXTCHAR. If either of them contains a blank or a punctuation mark, then write a value to NEWCMNT that contains the full 20 characters. Take no additional action and allow the automatic output at the bottom of the DATA step to write an observation with the current value of NEWCMNT.

```
   if cutpt in (' ',',',';','.','?','!') or
      nextchar in (' ',',',';','.','?','!') then
         do;
             newcomnt=substr(comments,1,20);
         end;
```

If the previous condition is not true, then NEWCOMNT ends in the middle of a word. Read backwards through the string until reaching a blank or a punctuation mark. Assign the new shorter value to NEWCOMNT. An observation with this new value for NEWCOMNT is written to data set NEW automatically.

```
   else do;
      do i=19 to 1 by -1 until (cutpt in (' ',',',';','.','?','!'));
         cutpt=substr(comments,i,1);
      end;
      newcomnt=substr(comments,1,i);
   end;
run;
```

Example 6.9

Creating SAS Datetime Values

Goal

Create a new variable that contains a SAS datetime value from a variable that contains a SAS date value and a variable that contains a SAS time value.

Strategy

Use the DHMS function to combine a SAS date value and a SAS time value into a single SAS datetime value.

Input Data Sets

In data set ONE, DATEVAL contains a SAS date value and TIMEVAL contains a SAS time value.

```
              ONE

OBS      DATEVAL     TIMEVAL

  1     19JUL1994    16:00:00
  2     25DEC1994    14:22:05
  3     01JAN1995    23:01:00
  4     09JAN1995     9:35:01
```

Resulting Data Set

Output 6.9   RESULTS Data Set

```
                    RESULTS

         OBS        DATIMVAL

          1     19JUL94:16:00:00
          2     25DEC94:14:22:05
          3     01JAN95:23:01:00
          4     09JAN95:09:35:01
```

Program

Create RESULTS. Read an observation from ONE.

Create a new variable, DATIMVAL, to contain a SAS datetime value. The DHMS function returns a SAS datetime value from numeric values that represent the date, hour, minute, and second. Because the values of TIMEVAL are SAS time values and these values contain the number of seconds since the previous midnight, it is not necessary for the hour and minute arguments to have a value. Zeros are used in their place and the time variable TIMEVAL is used for the seconds argument. The FORMAT statement permanently associates the DATETIME. format with DATIMVAL so that it will always display in that format.

The objective is to use a SAS date value and a SAS time value to create a new variable that contains a datetime value. The DHMS function accepts four numeric values that provide values for date, hour, minute, and seconds, respectively. It returns a single value in the form of a SAS datetime value. In this example, the DATEVAL variable supplies the date value and the TIMEVAL variable supplies the time, which is stored as an integer representing the number of seconds since midnight:

```
data results(keep=datimval);
   set one;

   datimval=dhms(dateval,0,0,timeval);
   format datimval datetime.;
run;
```

Where to Go from Here

□ **SAS datetime values.** For a complete discussion of how SAS handles time, date, and datetime values, see "Using SAS Date and Time Values" on p. 85 and "Understanding SAS Date and Time Values" on pp. 129–131 in *SAS Language: Reference, Version 6, First Edition.*

Example 6.10

Creating a SAS Time Value from a Character Value

Goal

Read a character value to create a SAS time value.

Strategy

Converting a character value to a SAS time value is a multistep process if the value is not in a form that can be read with an existing SAS time informat or function, such as the TIME*n*. informat or the HMS function. If the data values are not in such a form, you must first create a picture format that is in the form expected by the SAS informat TIME11 (or HMS function). Then use a series of assignment statements that contain INPUT and PUT functions to transform a character value into a numeric value and then into a SAS time value.

Input Data Sets

TIME1 contains the character variable TIMECHAR.

```
          TIME1

OBS    TIMECHAR

 1     33.49
 2     1:13.69
 3     13:00:00.33
 4     1:13:43.45
```

Resulting Data Set

Output 6.10   TIME2 Data Set

```
                    TIME2
     OBS      SASTIME      TIMECHAR

      1      0:00:33.49    33.49
      2      0:01:13.69    1:13.69
      3     13:00:00.33    13:00:00.33
      4      1:13:43.45    1:13:43.45
```

Program

The objective is to create a SAS time value from the character value TIMECHAR in data set TIME1. First, use the PICTURE statement in PROC FORMAT to create a user-defined format that you will use later to put a value into the proper form for a SAS time value (*hours:minutes:seconds*) so that it can be read with the TIME11. informat.

Use the COMPRESS function to remove the colons from the values of TIMECHAR. Then read this value with the INPUT function and a numeric informat to return a numeric value that can be written with a picture format. Use the PUT function and a picture format to write the numeric value to variable TEMP2, so that it can be read as a SAS time value with the TIME11. informat and assigned to a variable named SASTIME. As an example, a value that contains only seconds and tenths of seconds (33.34), will be expanded to contain leading zeros for hours and minutes (00:00:33.34).

The value that is assigned to SASTIME is not only numeric, it is also a valid SAS time value. For example, the SASTIME value that prints as 13:00:00:33 is stored as 46800.33.

Create the TME. format. Use the PICTURE statement to create a format that can be used as a template for writing numbers. In this case, the format will be used to write a value so that it can be read as a SAS time value.

```
proc format;
    picture tme other='99:99:99.99' ;
run;
```

Create TIME2. Permanently associate the TIME11.2 format with the new variable SASTIME. Read an observation from TIME1.

```
data time2(drop=temp1 temp2);
    format sastime time11.2;
    set time1;
```

Create a SAS time value and assign it to the new variable SASTIME. The COMPRESS function returns the value of TIMECHAR without the colons, and the assignment statement assigns the new value to TEMP1. In the second assignment statement, TEMP2 is assigned a character value as the result of two functions. The INPUT function returns a numeric value by reading the character value TEMP1 with the numeric informat 11.2. The PUT function then returns a character value written with the user-defined format TME. The last assignment statement assigns a valid SAS time value to SASTIME by using the INPUT function to read the value of TEMP2 with the TIME11. informat.

```
    temp1=compress(timechar,':');
    temp2=put(input(temp1,11.2),tme.);
    sastime=input(temp2,time11.);
run;
```

Where to Go from Here

□ **PROC FORMAT and the PICTURE statement.**

   □ For complete reference information and examples see Chapter 18, "The FORMAT Procedure," in *SAS Procedures Guide, Version 6, Third Edition.*

   □ For another example, see pp. 356–358 in *SAS Language and Procedures: Usage 2, Version 6, First Edition.*

   □ For an example of eliminating the leading zeros on numbers between zero and one, see the Input/Output article by Philip Shelton and Jason Sharpe, *Observations,* Fourth Quarter 1993, 57–60.

□ **INPUT and PUT functions.** For a complete reference information on these functions, see Chapter 11, "SAS Functions," in *SAS Language: Reference, Version 6, First Edition.* For numerous examples and explanations, see *SAS Language and Procedures: Usage 2, Version 6, First Edition.*

□ **SAS date and time values.** For a complete discussion of how SAS handles time, date, and datetime values, see "Using SAS Date and Time Values" on p. 85 and "Understanding SAS Date and Time Values" on pp. 129–131 in *SAS Language: Reference, Version 6, First Edition.*

Example 6.11

Calculating a Person's Age

Goal

Determine a person's current age using their date of birth.

Strategy

Determine the current age of each person in a data set by subtracting the SAS data value of the date of birth from the current date. Use the TODAY function to obtain the SAS date value of the current date. Use the INTCK function to count the number of months between the date of birth and the current date. Divide the number of months by 12 to produce the number of years. Use the MONTH function to determine if the month of the birthday and the current date are the same. If they are, determine if the birthday has occurred this year. If it hasn't, adjust the age by subtracting one year.

Input Data Sets

BIRTH

OBS	NAME	BDAY
1	Miguel	December 31, 1973
2	Joe	February 28, 1976
3	Rutger	March 29, 1976
4	Broguen	March 1, 1976
5	Susan	December 12, 1976
6	Michael	February 14, 1971
7	LeCe	November 9, 1967
8	Hans	July 2, 1955
9	Lou	July 30, 1960

Resulting Data Set

Output 6.11   AGES Data Set

AGES

OBS	NAME	BDAY	CURRENT	AGE
1	Miguel	December 31, 1973	July 10, 1995	21
2	Joe	February 28, 1976	July 10, 1995	19
3	Rutger	March 29, 1976	July 10, 1995	19
4	Broguen	March 1, 1976	July 10, 1995	19
5	Susan	December 12, 1976	July 10, 1995	18
6	Michael	February 14, 1971	July 10, 1995	24
7	LeCe	November 9, 1967	July 10, 1995	27
8	Hans	July 2, 1955	July 10, 1995	40
9	Lou	July 30, 1960	July 10, 1995	34

Program

The objective is to determine the current age of each person in data set BIRTH. Use the TODAY function in an assignment statement to assign the value of the current date to CURRENT. Use the INTCK function to return the number of months between the person's date of birth and the current date. If the birth month and the current month are the same, adjust for the fact that the birthday may not yet have occurred. Use the MONTH function to return the month from each date and the DAY function to return the day from each date:

Create AGES. Read an observation from BIRTH.

```
data ages;
   set birth;
```

Set CURRENT to a SAS date value representing today's date. Assign a SAS date format to CURRENT. It is always advisable to associate a format with a date value.

```
   current=today();
   format current worddate20.;
```

Assign a value to AGE. The INTCK function calculates and returns the number of month intervals between a person's date of birth and the current date. After that number is divided by 12 to produce the age in years, the INT function returns the integer portion.

```
   age=int(intck('month',bday,current)/12);
```

When the current month is the same as the birth month, adjust the value of age, based on whether the birthday has occurred. The MONTH function returns a value between 1 and 12 that represents the month of the current date value of BDAY and CURRENT. When adjusting the value of AGE, the assignment statement uses Boolean logic to return a value of 0 or 1. If the day of the month for BDAY is greater than CURRENT, then the birthday has not yet occurred, so a value of 1 is subtracted from AGE. If the birthday has occured, a value of 0 is substracted from AGE.

```
   if month(bday)=month(current) then
      age=age-(day(bday)>day(current));
run;
```

A P P E N D I X
Error Checking When Using MODIFY or SET with KEY=

Why Error Checking?

When reading observations with the SET statement and KEY= option or with the MODIFY statement, error checking is imperative for several reasons. The most important reason is that because these tools use nonsequential access methods, there is no guarantee that an observation will be located that satisfies the request. Error checking enables you to direct execution to specific paths, depending on the outcome of the I/O operation. Your program will continue execution for expected conditions and terminate execution when unexpected results occur.

New Error-Checking Tools

Two tools have been created to make error checking easier when you use the MODIFY statement or the SET statement with the KEY= option to process SAS data sets:

☐   _IORC_ automatic variable

☐   SYSRC autocall macro.

IORC is created automatically when you use the MODIFY statement or the SET statement with KEY=. The value of _IORC_ is a numeric return code that indicates the status of the I/O operation from the most recently executed MODIFY or SET statement with KEY=. Checking the value of this variable for abnormal I/O conditions enables you to detect them and direct execution down specific code paths instead of having the application terminate abnormally. For example, if the KEY= variable value does match between two observations, you might want to combine them and output an observation. If they don't match, however, you may want only to write a note to the log.

Because the values of the _IORC_ automatic variable are internal and subject to change, the SYSRC macro was created to enable you to test for specific I/O conditions while protecting your code from future changes in _IORC_ values. Using SYSRC, you can check the value of _IORC_ by specifying one of the mnemonics listed in Table A.1.

Table A.1 List of Most Common Mnemonic Values of _IORC_ for DATA Step Processing

Mnemonic Value	Meaning of Return Code
_DSENMR	The TRANSACTION data set observation does not exist in the MASTER data set. (This return code occurs when MODIFY with BY is used and no match occurs.)
_DSEMTR	Multiple TRANSACTION data set observations with the same BY variable value do not exist in the MASTER data set. (This return code occurs when MODIFY with BY is used and consecutive observations with the same BY values do not find a match in the first data set. In this situation, the first observation to fail to find a match returns _DSENMR. Following ones return _DSEMTR.)
_DSENOM	No matching observation was found in MASTER data set. (This return code occurs when SET or MODIFY with KEY= finds no match.)
_SOK	The I/O operation was successful. (This return code occurs when a match is found.)

Example 1: Routing Execution When an Unexpected Condition Occurs

This example shows how to prevent an unexpected condition from terminating the DATA step. The goal is to update a master data set with new information from a transaction data set. This application assumes that there are no duplicate values for the common variable in either data set.[*]

Input Data Sets

The TRANS data set contains three observations: two updates to information in MASTER and a new observation about PARTNO value 6 that needs to be added. MASTER is indexed on PARTNO. There are no duplicate values of PARTNO in MASTER or TRANS.

```
           MASTER                             TRANS

OBS    PARTNO    QUANTITY           OBS    PARTNO    ADDQUANT

 1        1         10               1        4         14
 2        2         20               2        6         16
 3        3         30               3        2         12
 4        4         40
 5        5         50
```

---

[*] This program works as expected only if the master and transaction data sets contain no consecutive observations with the same value for the common variable. For an explanation of the behavior of MODIFY with KEY= when duplicates exist, see SAS Technical Report P-242, *SAS Software: Changes and Enhancements, Release 6.08*, pages 4 and 8–10.

Correctly Updated MASTER Data Set

Output A.1a MASTER Data Set

MASTER contains updated quantities for PARTNO values 2 and 4 and a new observation for PARTNO value 6.

```
                         MASTER

            OBS      PARTNO      QUANTITY

             1         1           10
             2         2           32
             3         3           30
             4         4           54
             5         5           50
             6         6           16
```

Original Program

The objective is to update the MASTER data set with information from the TRANS data set. The program reads TRANS sequentially. MASTER is read directly, not sequentially, using the MODIFY statement and the KEY= option. Only observations with matching values for PARTNO, the KEY= variable, are read from MASTER.

Open MASTER for update. Read an observation from TRANS. Match observations from MASTER based on the values of PARTNO. Update the information on QUANTITY by adding the new values from TRANS.

```
data master;
   set trans;
   modify master key=partno;
   quantity = quantity + addquant;
run;
```

Resulting Log

Output A.1b Log Message about DATA Step Ending

This program has correctly updated one observation but stopped when it could not find a match for PARTNO value 6.

```
ERROR: No matching observation was found in MASTER data set.
PARTNO=6 ADDQUANT=16 QUANTITY=70 _ERROR_=1 _IORC_=1230015 _N_=2
NOTE: The SAS System stopped processing this step because of errors.
NOTE: The data set WORK.MASTER has been updated.  There were 1
      observations rewritten, 0 observations added and 0 observations
      deleted.
```

Resulting Data Set

Output A.1c Incorrectly Updated MASTER

The updated master has five observations. One observation was updated correctly, a new one was not added, and a second update was not made.

```
                         MASTER

            OBS      PARTNO      QUANTITY

             1         1           10
             2         2           20
             3         3           30
             4         4           54
             5         5           50
```

Revised Program

Open MASTER for update. Read an observation from TRANS. Match observations from MASTER based on the value of PARTNO.

Take the correct course of action based on whether a matching value for PARTNO is found in MASTER. Update QUANTITY by adding the new values from TRANS. The SELECT group directs execution to the correct code. When a match occurs (_SOK), update QUANTITY and replace the original observation in MASTER. When there is no match (_DSENOM), set QUANTITY equal to the ADDQUANT amount from TRANS, and append a new observation. _ERROR_ is reset to 0 to prevent an error condition that would write the contents of the program data vector to the SAS log. When an unexpected condition occurs, write messages and the contents of the program data vector to the log, and stop the DATA step.

The objective is to apply two updates and one addition to MASTER, preventing the DATA step from stopping when it does not find a match in MASTER for the PARTNO value 6 in TRANS. By adding error checking, this DATA step is allowed to complete normally and produce a correctly revised version of MASTER. This program uses the _IORC_ automatic variable and the SYSRC autocall macro in a SELECT group to check the value of the _IORC_ variable and execute the appropriate code based on whether or not a match is found.

```
data master;
   set trans;
   modify master key=partno;

   select(_iorc_);
      when(%sysrc(_sok)) do;
         quantity = quantity + addquant;
         replace;
      end;
      when(%sysrc(_dsenom)) do;
         quantity = addquant;
         _error_ = 0;
         output;
      end;
      otherwise do;
         put 'ERROR: Unexpected value for _IORC_= ' _iorc_;
         put 'Program terminating. Data step iteration # ' _n_;
         put _all_;
         stop;
      end;
   end;
run;
```

Resulting Log

Output A.1d Log Message

The DATA step executed without error and observations were appropriately updated and added.

```
NOTE: The data set WORK.MASTER has been updated.  There were 2
      observations rewritten, 1 observations added and 0 observations
      deleted.
```

See the correctly updated version of MASTER in Output A.1a.

Example 2: Using Error Checking on *All* Statements That Use KEY=

This example shows how important it is to use error checking on *all* statements that use the KEY= option when reading data.

Input Data Sets

The MASTER and DESCRPTN data sets are both indexed on PARTNO. The ORDER data set contains values for all parts in a single order. Only ORDER contains the PARTNO value 8.

	MASTER			ORDER	
OBS	PARTNO	QUANTITY		OBS	PARTNO
1	1	10		1	2
2	2	20		2	4
3	3	30		3	1
4	4	40		4	3
5	5	50		5	8
				6	5
				7	6

	DESCRPTN	
OBS	PARTNO	DESC
1	4	nuts
2	3	bolts
3	2	screws
4	6	washers

Correctly Created COMBINE Data Set

Output A.2a   COMBINE Data Set

Note that COMBINE does not contain an observation with the PARTNO value 8. This value does not occur in either MASTER or DESCRPTN.

		COMBINE	
OBS	PARTNO	DESC	QUANTITY
1	2	screws	20
2	4	nuts	40
3	1	No description	10
4	3	bolts	30
5	5	No description	50
6	6	washers	0

Original Program

The objective is to create a data set that contains the description and number in stock for each part in a single order, except for the parts that are not found in either of the two input data sets, MASTER and DESCRPTN. A transaction data set contains the part numbers of all parts in a single order. One data set is read to retrieve the description of the part and another is read to retrieve the quantity in stock.

The program reads the ORDER data set sequentially and then uses SET with the KEY= option to read the MASTER and DESCRPTN data sets directly, based on the key value of PARTNO. When a match occurs, an observation is written that contains all the necessary information for each value of PARTNO in ORDER. This first attempt at a solution uses error checking for only one of the two SET statements that use KEY= to read a data set.

Create COMBINE. Read an observation from ORDER. Read an observation from DESCRPTN and one from MASTER based on a matching value for PARTNO, the key variable. Note that no error checking occurs after an observation is read from DESCRPTN.

Take the correct course of action, based on whether a matching value for PARTNO is found in MASTER or DESCRPTN. (This logic is based on the erroneous assumption that this SELECT group performs error checking for both of the preceding SET statements that contain the KEY= option. It actually performs error checking for only the most recent one.) The SELECT group directs execution to the correct code. When a match occurs (_SOK), the value of PARTNO in the observation being read from MASTER matches the current PARTNO value from ORDER. So, output an observation. When there is no match (_DSENOM), no observations in MASTER contain the current value of PARTNO, so set the value of DESC appropriately and output an observation. _ERROR_ is reset to 0 to prevent an error condition that would write the contents of the program data vector to the SAS log. When an unexpected condition occurs, write messages and the contents of the program data vector to the log, and stop the DATA step.

```
data combine;
   set order;
   set descrptn key=partno;
   set master key=partno;



   select(_iorc_);
      when(%sysrc(_sok)) do;
         output;
      end;
      when(%sysrc(_dsenom)) do;
         desc = 'No description';
         _error_ = 0;
         output;
      end;
      otherwise do;
         put 'ERROR: Unexpected value for _IORC_= ' _iorc_;
         put 'Program terminating.';
         put _all_;
         stop;
      end;
   end;
run;
```

Resulting Log

Output A.2b Log Message

This program creates an output data set but executes with one error.

```
PARTNO=1 DESC=nuts QUANTITY=10 _ERROR_=1 _IORC_=0 _N_=3
PARTNO=5 DESC=No description QUANTITY=50 _ERROR_=1 _IORC_=0 _N_=6
NOTE: The data set WORK.COMBINE has 7 observations and 3 variables.
```

Resulting Data Set

Output A.2c Incorrectly Created
COMBINE

Observation 5 should not be in this data set.
PARTNO value 8 does not exist in either
MASTER or DESC, so no QUANTITY
should be listed for it. Also, observations 3
and 7 contain descriptions from
observations 2 and 6, respectively.

```
                           COMBINE

        OBS    PARTNO    DESC            QUANTITY
         1       2       screws            20
         2       4       nuts              40
         3       1       nuts              10
         4       3       bolts             30
         5       8       No description    30
         6       5       No description    50
         7       6       No description    50
```

Revised Program

*Create COMBINE. Read an observation
from ORDER. Read an observation from
DESCRPTN, using PARTNO as the key
variable.* FOUNDES is created so that its
value can be used later to indicate when a
PARTNO value has a match in
DESCRPTN.

*Take the correct course of action based on
whether a matching value for PARTNO is
found in DESCRPTN.* The SELECT group
directs execution to the correct code based
on the value of _IORC_. When a match
occurs (_SOK), the value of PARTNO in
the observation being read from
DESCRPTN matches the current value
from ORDER. FOUNDES is set to 1 to
indicate that DESCRPTN contributed to the
current observation. When there is no match
(_DSENOM), no observations in
DESCRPTN contain the current value of
PARTNO, so the description is set
appropriately. _ERROR_ is reset to 0 to
prevent an error condition that would write
the contents of the program data vector to
the SAS log. Any other _IORC_ value
indicates that an unexpected condition has
been met, so messages are written to the log
and the DATA step is stopped.

To create an accurate output data set, this example performs error checking on
both SET statements that use the KEY= option:

```
data combine(drop=foundes);
   set order;
   foundes = 0;
   set descrptn key=partno;



   select(_iorc_);
      when(%sysrc(_sok)) do;
         foundes = 1;
      end;
      when(%sysrc(_dsenom)) do;
         desc = 'No description';
         _error_ = 0;
      end;
      otherwise do;
         put 'ERROR: Unexpected value for _IORC_= ' _iorc_;
         put 'Program terminating. Data set accessed is DESCRPTN';
         put _all_;
         _error_ = 0;
         stop;
      end;
   end;
```

***Read an observation from MASTER,
using PARTNO as a key variable.***

```
set master key=partno;
```

***Take the correct course of action based on
whether a matching value for PARTNO is
found in MASTER.*** When a match is found
(_SOK) between the current PARTNO
value from ORDER and from MASTER,
write an observation. When a match isn't
found (_DSENOM) in MASTER, test the
value of FOUNDES. If FOUNDES is not
true, then a value wasn't found in
DESCRPTN either, so write a message to
the log but do not write an observation. If
FOUNDES is true, however, the value is in
DESCRPTN but not MASTER. So write an
observation but set QUANTITY to 0.
Again, if an unexpected condition occurs,
write a message and stop the DATA step.

```
select(_iorc_);
    when(%sysrc(_sok)) do;
        output;
    end;
    when(%sysrc(_dsenom)) do;
        if not foundes then do;
            _error_ = 0;
            put 'WARNING: PARTNO ' partno 'is not in'
                ' DESCRPTN or MASTER.';
        end;
        else do;
            quantity = 0;
            _error_ = 0;
            output;
        end;
    end;
    otherwise do;
        put 'ERROR: Unexpected value for _IORC_= ' _iorc_;
        put 'Program terminating. Data set accessed is MASTER';
        put _all_;
        _error_ = 0;
        stop;
    end;
end;       /* ends the SELECT group */
```

Resulting Log

Output A.2d Log Message

The DATA step executed without error. Six
observations were correctly created and a
message was written to the log.

```
WARNING: PARTNO 8 is not in DESCRPTN or MASTER.
NOTE: The data set WORK.COMBINE has 6 observations and 3 variables.
```

See the correctly created version of COMBINE in Output A.2a.

Index

Your Turn

If you have comments or suggestions about *Combining and Modifying SAS Data Sets: Examples, Version 6, First Edition*, please send them to us on a photocopy of this page or send us electronic mail.

For comments about this book, please return the photocopy to

> SAS Institute Inc.
> Publications Division
> SAS Campus Drive
> Cary, NC 27513
> **email:** yourturn@unx.sas.com

For suggestions about the software, please return the photocopy to

> SAS Institute Inc.
> Technical Support Division
> SAS Campus Drive
> Cary, NC 27513
> **email:** suggest@unx.sas.com